My Life Before

My Life Before

Memoir of a Lost Royal

Terrell Frazier

My Life Before

Copyright © 2019 by Terrell Frazier. All rights reserved.

No part of this publication may be reproduced, stored in a retrieval system or transmitted in any way by any means, electronic, mechanical, photocopy, recording or otherwise without the prior permission of the author except as provided by USA copyright law.

The opinions expressed by the author are not necessarily those of URLink Print and Media.

1603 Capitol Ave., Suite 310 Cheyenne, Wyoming USA 82001
1-888-980-6523 | admin@urlinkpublishing.com

URLink Print and Media is committed to excellence in the publishing industry.

Book design copyright © 2019 by URLink Print and Media. All rights reserved.

Published in the United States of America
ISBN 978-1-64367-496-4 (Paperback)
ISBN 978-1-64367-495-7 (Digital)

30.04.19

My Life Before

Memoir of a Lost Royal

Terrell Frazier

My Life Before

Copyright © 2019 by Terrell Frazier. All rights reserved.

No part of this publication may be reproduced, stored in a retrieval system or transmitted in any way by any means, electronic, mechanical, photocopy, recording or otherwise without the prior permission of the author except as provided by USA copyright law.

The opinions expressed by the author are not necessarily those of URLink Print and Media.

1603 Capitol Ave., Suite 310 Cheyenne, Wyoming USA 82001
1-888-980-6523 | admin@urlinkpublishing.com

URLink Print and Media is committed to excellence in the publishing industry.

Book design copyright © 2019 by URLink Print and Media. All rights reserved.

Published in the United States of America

ISBN 978-1-64367-496-4 (Paperback)
ISBN 978-1-64367-495-7 (Digital)

30.04.19

Contents

My Life Before 7
To My Beloveds...9
Introduction..11
The Trigger 15
The Doors reopen 18
Sunset at Amarna 23
Meeting Pharoah Seti I..38
Love One's Lost...54
"A New Era Has Been Born" 75
"The Secret Chamber" 79
The Crushing Moment 84
"Enough is enough" 89
Irem: battle between Lovers...97
"Aftermath" 102
Mehy: The Love Song 116
Music to my soul...118
Movie Madness 124
Stature of Peace 127
Glossary 135
Hopes for a Bright Future 141

MY LIFE BEFORE

This story is about the topic of reincarnation, about a life that I believed I once lived in a time long ago. The persons that I've named throughout this story are actual people whom lived long ago, people whom I believed to be my relatives in my past life and people whom become acquainted with and fell in love with. All research and identifications of these persons has been done long after majority of these memories were revived. It is up to you if you want to believe in my story or not but I just want someone to listen what I have to say first before you rule me out as a crazed fraud or worse. Reincarnation wasn't one of my original beliefs. "No one can come back to life" I thought to myself and what I was always taught, but because of these visions, my beliefs, and everything that was taught to me changed.

To My Beloveds

To my niece, nephews and those who would follow know who you are be who you are."

To my dearest Past life sisters; Meritaten (pronounced Mery-aten), Ankhesenpa'aten (pronounced Ankh- e-sen-pa-aten), Tenta'aten (pronounced Ten-ta-aten), Neferneferuaten-Tasherit (pronounced Nefer-nefer-aten Ta-she-rit), Nefernerferure (pronounced Nefer-nefer-ure), Setepenre (pronounced Sotep-enre), and my aunt Beketaten *(pronounced Beke-aten), because all in all, my story is your story. Finally, at last your cries, my cries, can be heard. You were my everything in my past life and still are in this present.*

To my current siblings, I feel like we are something important as well. Allow this story to influence you and encourage to be the best you can be and be very proud of where you come from. Despite if you all believe this or not you all are descendants of power kings of queens who graced all of Africa with their very being. Be proud of who you are and stay true to who you are as well.

To Tutankhamun, oh how could I forget about you. May your soul finally rest in peace, may you sleep well in your tomb and your spirit sour high above and around the Aten, rest in peace my dear ancestor.

Thirdly, I would also like to dedicate this story to my mother. The world has seemed to have forgotten about you and I know it seems like you that you're not living up to your expectations. I'm hoping that this story could restore the honor that you once held. I wear you in my heart and soul. You are my crown that shines so bright my signature that says that I'm the son of a queen thus mommy a queen whom may have lost her way but has been found. Mother you are my flames that ignite my dignity and my prideful strut, I held my head strong and high because of you. Although there have been many times in which you and I didn't get along, I still love you no matter what.

To all of my family relatives, I know that you also feel as though you all aren't living at your own expectations, or not proud of your lives. But, just look at your family background, you all descended from powerful Kings and Queens, that's something to be proud and empowered by, I know I am. Hell, even though most of you get my damn nerves, I'm not ashamed of you. I rather have you all as a family than some rich lifeless family. So be empowered by our ancestors and keep strong.

The last person that I want to dedicate this book to is I. Terrell for a long time now, you've walked in the shadows questioning your very being and feeling sorry for yourself. It's time to stop doing so. You are not a monster as you are led to believe by others and worse, yourself. You should be proud of your accomplishments and how far you have come become, you could have really remained dead to the world. Live happy, be happy, and stop telling yourself you can't, because you can do a lot. I'm so proud of you

To My Beloveds

To my niece, nephews and those who would follow know who you are be who you are."

To my dearest Past life sisters; Meritaten (pronounced Mery-aten), Ankhesenpa'aten (pronounced Ankh- e-sen-pa-aten), Tenta'aten (pronounced Ten-ta-aten), Neferneferuaten-Tasherit (pronounced Nefer-nefer-aten Ta-she-rit), Nefernerferure (pronounced Nefer-nefer-ure), Setepenre (pronounced Sotep-enre), and my aunt Beketaten (pronounced Beke-aten), because all in all, my story is your story. Finally, at last your cries, my cries, can be heard. You were my everything in my past life and still are in this present.

To my current siblings, I feel like we are something important as well. Allow this story to influence you and encourage to be the best you can be and be very proud of where you come from. Despite if you all believe this or not you all are descendants of power kings of queens who graced all of Africa with their very being. Be proud of who you are and stay true to who you are as well.

To Tutankhamun, oh how could I forget about you. May your soul finally rest in peace, may you sleep well in your tomb and your spirit sour high above and around the Aten, rest in peace my dear ancestor.

Thirdly, I would also like to dedicate this story to my mother. The world has seemed to have forgotten about you and I know it seems like you that you're not living up to your expectations. I'm hoping that this story could restore the honor that you once held. I wear you in my heart and soul. You are my crown that shines so bright my signature that says that I'm the son of a queen thus mommy a queen whom may have lost her way but has been found. Mother you are my flames that ignite my dignity and my prideful strut, I held my head strong and high because of you. Although there have been many times in which you and I didn't get along, I still love you no matter what.

To all of my family relatives, I know that you also feel as though you all aren't living at your own expectations, or not proud of your lives. But, just look at your family background, you all descended from powerful Kings and Queens, that's something to be proud and empowered by, I know I am. Hell, even though most of you get my damn nerves, I'm not ashamed of you. I rather have you all as a family than some rich lifeless family. So be empowered by our ancestors and keep strong.

The last person that I want to dedicate this book to is I. Terrell for a long time now, you've walked in the shadows questioning your very being and feeling sorry for yourself. It's time to stop doing so. You are not a monster as you are led to believe by others and worse, yourself. You should be proud of your accomplishments and how far you have come become, you could have really remained dead to the world. Live happy, be happy, and stop telling yourself you can't, because you can do a lot. I'm so proud of you

INTRODUCTION

"I am my own ancestor"

Hello everyone, I'm Terrell Leonardo Frazier, the person who is telling you this story, or should I say memoir of my life, of my past life. On June 11th, 1990, I was reincarnated back on earth, born to Tabatha Shameka Frazier and Steven Curtis Thompson. At the point in time, I have just come from another lifetime from being the mixed son, of a wealthy slave master, whom lived in the late 1800s. My name was Jr. I had five older half- brothers who were slaves the oldest being known as Terrence. That life in those times was my very first experience with the past lives experience, but that is another story, for a different time and book.

This epic story is about a past life that I believed that I once lived in Ancient Egypt during the late 18th and early 19th dynasties of Egypt, the times of the famous boy king, King Tut and the pharaoh Seti I. But, that's not all. I also believed that I was and still, a lost relative to Tutankhamun. My reasons I will share with you later on in the chapters. I've told many about my experience some were ignorant to my beliefs and some chose to be oblivious to them. I assumed that since this was a different time and era that people would be more open to what I believed, but I was wrong, completely wrong. However, that didn't stop me from pushing forward in my beliefs. I wasn't giving these memories for no reason. If I was going to believe in and make others see what I saw I was going to have to go head strong.

The reason why I chose to right about my past life in Egypt is because it's the life that still very fresh in my mind, and in my opinion, it holds some valuable info to Egyptology, which may help solve many of the questions surrounding the late 18th dynasty King and Queens. My story is very dear to me because without these occurrences ever even happening to me, I would not be the half the man I am today; I would still be a lost soul trying to find out who I am and where I hailed from. I'm so grateful that this ever happened to me

What I'm about to share with all of you readers, is an experience that I encountered during my late teens and early twenties. Unlike my first experience, it took a vast amount of years to recall these memories, which is another reason why I felt like these memories should be shared with the entire world.

What happened to me, in this experience, whether it was physical or spiritual, has changed my whole outlook about life. So many of my answers, which I've had about what happens to us after we die, have been answered. I know now why some things happen to some people. I also understand a little more about life, and I'm dying to know more. Still, I want to know more of what's in store for me every day as I carry on in this life. You can say this book is my memoir, a memoir of lifelong passed. From my birth to my death, I'm about to share with you, the readers all everything about whom I once was and where I came from, thus how I died, and beyond my death. It's an unsteady road so please keep your balance.

For those of you, who don't know what Reincarnation is, it's the belief that a person's spirit, or soul is reborn as new human being, or animal after their previous death. For thousands of years, thousands of people all over the world, believed in reincarnation and some have shared their experiences about past lives, just like I'm sharing mine with you readers. In the Hindu belief, one is reincarnated through Karma, if one does something bad in he or she's current life, he or she will pay for that deed in the next life. Well, I have to say, based upon my experience, that the Hindus are so right. Karma and reincarnation is very real.

Not only does a person have one past life, but he or she can have multiple past lives as well. It's unclear how many lives that I've lived. So far, I could only recall most memories from only two of them. Yet, one night, I was shown many events from the past that I believe came from each of my past lives.

In one life, I saw myself hiding in a very dark room, which appeared to be a closet with several other young boys. It seems as though if we each were placed inside this pitch black room by an evil Roman ruler, who wanted to kill each one of us. Only I managed to escape this evil ruler's wrath and fled to another area where this ruler couldn't get his hands on me.

The next memory was of me being a very beautiful a blonde woman. From the vision stand point, I looked as if I was a settler from the Westerns of American. Next, I saw myself running across a huge valley for some unknown reasons. Then, I saw myself as a runaway slave, hiding behind a tree from white settlers; I was creeping slowly and quietly from the settlers, attempting to find my way to freedom. Could all of these events be moments of my past? The answer, I suspected was yes. I was remembering all those times at once.

It appeared to me, that in every one of those lives, I was running from something, which I find to be truthful in this life. Whenever there is a situation in which I couldn't handle, I'm quick to find an exit. Now, I'm learning that one can't solve a problem by running away. One must face up with this problem in a more sufficient way.

In my opinion, reincarnation happens when we are supposed to learn something that we maybe didn't learn quiet well or pick up in another lifetime. Reincarnation is a part of life and it's necessary, that way a person could learn from his or hers past mistakes, or to give our present self some sort of inspiration, which I think is the reason why my memories were restored.

Before all this, I thought there was no reason for my being, that I was a useless soul. But, because of my memoires, I know now that this self-lie isn't true. We, as humans, tend to think that this life that we are living now is a long road by itself. But, it turns out to be a road connected to a much longer road in which we are only at the halfway point to the end of the road.

God is not done with you when you die. There is a lot more in store for you in the afterlife. True, your psychical body, one's temple, as it's called, will no longer will be active but one's soul is eternal it never ceased. However, one gets a new temple if he or she is reincarnated. No, one doesn't look the same as one did before (sad but it's true). However, one may have the ability to recognized old friends, families, or even foes via their soul once one recall a memory from a past life. The bad part, is one might retain old wounds and sicknesses from your previous life like I have. I'm currently still injured rom the wound inflicted upon me by Seti. But, I believed that they come back to us so that they can be cured in the next life.

I've been asked several times by skeptics. "If reincarnation is real, then why would God send us back?" The simple answer to that is to learn. A tree cannot grow without the rain. This simply means to flourish one has to go throw some hardships, some rain, to become better in life. Our Lord might put you in a similar position, to whatever you have already gone through before in a past life, or even present life, to make you grow and to teach yourself, and even others, not to make those same mistakes.

Always remember, that you are here for a reason, and that reason is always good. The phrase, "God works in mysterious ways" is very true. I really wish that you readers can heed from my past mistakes and learn from them. I've learned more about me than I knew about myself from mistakes. One can do whatever one wants with this story. One can either believe it or one doesn't. But please listen to what I have to say.

Just one more thing before we start. Memories of a past life or lives don't start in the mind, as it is led to believe, by psychologist and skeptics. These memories come from the soul. You know, that place in the center of the chest, that very same place where God is said to communicate with one. This very same spot is what I call; the hallow. This hallow is the shell that holds are soul. These memories travels from the hallow, up into our brain, and goes off in our minds like a bomb. It's almost as if our brain is a movie projector, projecting long lost memories from times long past into our eyes. These memories come so strong and sometimes when you least expected to.

The Trigger

"Remember the Times"

It was August of 2008, my senior year of high school, it was just merely a week or two after school started back up again. I had a long day at school, and I was so tired and wanted to rest. Once I finished cleaning up my household duties in our new home, I took out my sheets and took a nap on the floor. It was hard to get any sleep with all the commotion that was going on in my house. I could hear by brothers and sister walking around the house, my mother frying chicken, and playing music. The music was so loud, that I could hear it in the back of the house where I was sleeping. One song that came on the channel was Michael Jackson's *"Remember the Time"*. This was one of my favorite Michael songs. This song had me dancing in my sleep, but then all the sudden I started to drift off to sleep, or whatever state I was in. After the dancing it was like my mind zapped to another location in time.

    Before I knew it, I was in Ancient Egypt, and Let me tell you, I wasn't dancing. A whole lot of events started happening before my very eyes. They began like a new movie trailer, you know when a new movie comes out and they show the certain parts of the movie in a trailer, well that's what happened in my vision. I could've felt the wind blowing on me, it was felt like I was being rushed through time or something like that.

All I remember from those events was me constantly calling out the name of "Seti!" to one of my high school classmates who dressed up like an Ancient Egyptian Pharaoh. Even though everything was going so fast, I managed to collect some of the key events and lock them in my mind.

At the end of the apparitions, this particular classmate impaled me in my left rib cage, after a battle in the dessert. Before I knew it, I popped up from my trance, or whatever the hell it was. To myself, I wondered why my classmate was wearing Egyptian clothing and why was I calling him Seti. Most of all, I wondered what this all meant. Freaky, ain't it.

Upon waking up, I looked to my clock to found out that I've been on the floor for at least an hour. "Wow!" I said to myself, in shock of the time frame. It was assumed that I've been lying there in that very spot for a few minutes; due to how fast everything was going in my premonition. Yet, the clock told me otherwise.

At first, I just thought it was some bad dream or something. But, then again, I remembered, I had something similar to this happen to me before. I knew good and well that this wasn't an ordinary dream but a memory of something. The first thing that came to mind was it was another past life experience. "Oh lord, not again" I chuckled. The last time I recalled memories of a past life they were very heart-wrenching and dark thus to go through that again was to me very a headache.

Certain things about these memories made me dismissed this whole situation. For one, I didn't even know that a person could have more than one life. I just assume that a person only has one. Secondly, I always thought that the ancient Egyptians weren't of African descent, but it turns out that I was totally wrong. They were black and brown just like the southern Africans of today.

After the incident, I immediately underwent some super intense massive research and discovered some startling facts that were shown to me in my memories. The most stunning of them all, was the instant discovery of The Pharaoh Seti. He was real, thus not a figment of my imagination. King Seti I. was the second Pharaoh of the 19th dynasty of Egypt and the father of Ramses the Great, the pharaoh most associated with the story of Exodus.

Seti's name meant, "He of Set" the ancient Egyptian god of darkness and chaos. Utterly shocked, my jaw dropped when Seti unearth to me on the internet.

"Oh my god!" I said to myself repeatedly in disbelief. The image of Seti really looked my classmate, from head to toe. Don't get me started when I saw his mummy, I was like.

"This is him" and "ooh he still looks handsome". To me, this was the key evidence that my dreams were actually the relocation of a past life, one that I lived a very long time ago.

Michael Jackson's song "Remember the Times" was the trigger that set off those old memories that were hidden deep in the back of my mind into motion. There was always the notion of doubt about my story being just a bad dream. But, the more this song came on the radio, the more I believed that the song played as a sign telling me remember, remember who you once were.

After the incident, I've told some of my closet friends, or people who I thought my friends about my experience and even the picture that of Seti, and I even told them who I thought he was. One of my friends didn't think that it looked like him. "How can you not see the similarities? The lips and the face" I said to myself in thought. Word did have gotten out about this to this classmate about this and he wasn't happy about this. "So much for trust" I said to myself. Man, did I felt like an idiot in that moment. After that, I never really trust anyone ever again let alone told someone about my experience.

My mouth remained shut for a few years afterwards and I seemed to have forgotten about the entire thing. I went on with my daily life, did the same daily things that I used to do. However, it wasn't long for these memories to come creeping back into my mind. This time they were going to come with full force with new memories and details of this alleged life I supposed I lived.

THE DOORS REOPEN

It was mid-summer of 2011; I was now in college studying to be a Graphic Designer at Trident Technical College. Man, I was trying so desperately to get the hell out of town, that I must have changed my major a thousand times trying to do so. At that point in time my life went to hell in a basket. Just a lot of shit happened to me that could have been avoided. Let's just say, I thought the whole world was my enemy, I hated everyone that I thought hated me or wanted to hurt me. A lot of people didn't know this, but I was suffering through depression.

All my life, I felt like no one wanted me around, or did not love me, and that I was seriously a mishap, because I couldn't do anything right and everything I tried to do right, I ended up doing totally wrong. People already hated me because I was an opened homosexual. In the beginning, not even my own mother approved of my lifestyle. This hurt me the most. I was virtually alone. Being black and gay was like being scum of the earth.

"You better not be a faggot" is what I grew up listening to and heeding with fear. But truly I didn't heed those hateful words because it was still inside me I couldn't get rid of these feelings. and it didn't take long for me to figure out who I was in this life. Truth be told I used to be a gay-bashing preacher in my life as Jr. but it looks like the tables has turned on me, so I guess part of the reason why I was here is because of Karma.

The gay bashing really ignited a hate in my soul for everyone whom used that to hurt me, but what really hit me the hardest was when I thought my father had other older children before me. Foolishly and stupidly, I was listening to he say she say, about my father being a "Rolling Stone" a whore and I believed those rumors. The two guys whom, I thought were my older brothers didn't even want anything to do with me because of my sexuality.

"Damn" I shouted out to myself, "if we are family we should love each other no matter what we felt was wrong with them". I cried out to myself.

I wouldn't have hated him if the shoes were on the other foot or even less give a damn. For years now, I've beaten myself up over and over again about the matter. I wanted to know who they were so damn bad, and I cared so much about them more than my own self. I've let myself go a lot because of this. It turned out that those two men didn't feel the same for me thus again, I was in heartbroken

I was literally a loveless human being. I didn't know what it was or how it felt all I knew was sex, and that was I thought was a key to love, but I was wrong. I've found myself literally looking for love for affection; putting myself out there like a prostitute. I got affection alright, but no love. I ruined my image putting myself out there like that, but back then; I thought I was having fun.

I would literally search for men to take me and place me in their big arms and fuck my brains out. I was a very horny toad as a friend called it and on top of that, I sunk into what all those negative people were saying about me.

I've ran into every single hater and gay basher that I met since childhood at Tech. Boy, did I fell into a den full of lions. These people still felt the same way about me as they did when we were younger. I was in a very bad position in that time of my life, very bad. It felt as though no one wanted me around or even cared for that matter that I was, I was so depressed so unhappy with my life, so distraught.

"Why was I here?" I would talk to the God of my understanding out loud and I was soon to find out why.

School didn't make anything better. Of course, I was the first male in my family to actually graduate High School and to attend college, but that didn't mean anything to me, because I didn't have my families love or that significant other in my life to make me feel that I was something special. For the most part, college was tough but there were some teachers that made it worth attending.

Favorite class in Trident Technical College was History 101. I had the funniest teacher ever. My history teacher always kept us laughing in class and her lectures were very enthusiastic. During the middle of the semester, my teacher had given us a term paper to write. We each were to a paper on someone or something of the past of our own choosing. My topic was on the famous Queen Nefertiti due to watching a documentary called "Nefertiti Resurrected" which aired on the History Channel a few weeks earlier. Nefertiti was a rough person to right about and I almost didn't want to do the essay on her, because it was so little to go on of the queen until one day, when I was doing my research, something unexpected happened.

As I watched the TV documentary, I began to receive unrelated visions from that time period in which Nefertiti lived. In this era, I was a toddler, a child of Akhenaten, the father of the famous boy king, Tutankhamen. I saw myself, as a toddler, running about in one of the Akhenaten's temples having a great time in what I now believe was my former life.

"Oh no no!" I said shaking my head trying to push the thoughts out of my head.

"This can't be happening, not again" I chuckled and laughed to myself while sitting at the computer.

But the more I shook, the more these images stuck in my head. The images were like paper to glue they were permanently stuck there. However, they weren't able to convince me they were real memories of my past life. So, I chose to ignore them again until something unexpected happened again. I was walking to the library and it was breezy out. As the breeze slapped my body with a sweet nice wind, I recalled the same feeling from being in the desert when In Egypt in my past life.

"What in the world?" I questioned" what was that about' as I continued walking down Sumter Avenue to the Library.

MY LIFE BEFORE

Not long after this, about a year later, familiar memories, the ones of Seti I and myself came sneaking up on me while I wasn't looking. It was on a grey evening and I was standing out on my porch, to get some fresh air and to be promiscuous, you know get some dick. The memories of Seti and I just popped up back in my head.

"What the hell?" I said to myself. "Why in the hell was this happening to me" I muttered to myself. It was unclear to me at the time, but right then and there I knew that it was time to put these memories into a book?

I knew instantly that the memories of being in Amarna as a child and the visions of me and King Seti were linked and I had to place them order and tell them the right way. It was a stretch because it seemed as though nothing made sense especially with all that have been recorded from these time eras. But my memories revealed that maybe the Egyptologists has something recorded wrong.

It took many years, sweat, and tears to get this story into shape. Even as I was writing this book, I couldn't shake away doubt from my inner thoughts. For years, I remained skeptical about my memories. The very thought of everyone criticizing my claims shook me with sharp great fear, but that all changed once I learned of a special person that had similar experience happened to her and her name was Omm Seti.

Omm Seti is a woman whom believed she was a priestess in her past life whom also had a relationship with King Seti. When I heard this, my jay dropped. For a moment, I thought I was going crazy thinking I was reincarnated from the past, but here Ohm Seti steps forward with her story and many believed her. This made me think if many people could listen to her, then they might hear me out. My only problem with this was the belief that people would think our two stories were identical but let me make this loud and clear. I NEVER HEARD OF OHM SETI BEFORE THESE EVENTS, EVER!

Ohm Seti's braveness to put her story forth gave me comfort within myself because I was scared, I was so afraid that everyone was going to mock me and denounce me but seeing how Ohm was willing to go forth with her story, gave me grace and the strength that I needed to push on with my story and I thank Ohm for that. Ohm has become my idol in this subject, and I appreciate what she has done a lot. Even though I knew little of her in this life, she and I may have actually crossed paths in the ancient times.

Sunset at Amarna

"I am Amenhotep born of Tadukhipa (Kiya) and her beloved Neferkheperure-Waenre (Akhenaten)".

More than three thousand years ago, on a bright and early day, a baby was being born, a royal child whom was to be born into a powerful dynasty the world has ever known, the 18th dynasty of Egypt. This child was me. The woman given birth to me was someone of great focus, even in that day and time. My mother was a very beautiful woman she had a smooth peanut butter skin and large lips. My mother skin was always shining like it was like marble and it always appeared to have shined in the sun.

My mother also wore this beautiful wig known as the Nubian wig, known to have been worn by the ancient Egyptians, especially within this time frame, which was the 18th dynasty of Egypt. What was also remarkable and surprising about Queen Kiya is that she held some striking parallels to my present day mother. The face the skin color, my mother skin also shines. At this point; I thought that the two persons were one and the same and it didn't take long for me to confirm that they were.

To some, my mother was known as Tadukhipa (pronounced Tad-uk-hipa) the daughter of king Tushratta (pronounced Tuushrat-ta) and Queen Juni of Mitanni, a small country northeastern to Egypt but by many, she was known as Queen Kiya, the secondary wife to the heretic pharaoh Akhenaten. For years, it was assumed that it was she whom was the mother of king Tut, but due to recent analysis, this theory has been ruled out. But, little did the scientist and archaeologist knew, that she was indeed the mother a prince, a prince that they have yet to knew about.

A lot of scholars have battled over the identity of Tadukhipa. To some she was the famous Queen Nefertiti, because the name Nefertiti in itself meant "the beautiful one has come" which made archaeologists' think that Nefertiti was the name given to the foreign princess upon her arrival to Egypt. The name Nefertiti is short for another name Neferneferutaen, which was Nefertiti's throne name. Tadukhipa was actually Akhenaten's secondary wife Kiya all in all; a little known queen but one will soon know this queen, personally.

I remember when I saw the famous carnopic jar depiction of Kiya (above). Immediately, I shook my head "yes." The face of the woman that was given birth to me, matched the face of Queen Kiya, and it was clear to me that she was indeed my mother in a past life. My mother still looks exactly like this amazing image. This beautiful sculpted image of Kiya is now the hallmark of my mother. I wave this image around like a flag every day.

It's believed by many Egyptologists that my mother vanished, or died during mid-years of my father's reign, but that was not so. What really happened was that all attention was placed upon the arrival of the first male heir in Tutankhamen pronounced *Toot-ank-amun*, otherwise known by all, king Tut. Tut's name meant "Living image of Amun" Amun being the Egyptian supreme God. So my mother was basically sidelined, but it wasn't long before she would found herself in the arms of my father again, because just few years later, she would conceive a son of her own, me.

This was a very special day for both my parents. A son was conceived out of their love. Upon my birth, my mother tickled me with a huge white feather and giggled as I cried in her arms. My Eldest aunt and my youngest aunt from my present life were also there. Either they were my mother's female attendants, or her sisters were unclear to me, but they were always around my mother everywhere she went. When my eldest aunt saw me, she had a great big smile on her face and so did my other aunt. My eldest aunt wore a very long Egyptian wig, much like my mother's wig and she wore a bright white gown.

"What are you going to name him?" my eldest aunt asked mother.

"Amenhotep (Amen-ho-tep)" mother responds as she smiled at me." After his father" she implied to her servant.

The name Amenhotep meant "Amun is satisfied". Amun was the chief Egyptian God. The name Amenhotep was very common in that time even some of my ancestor's names were Amenhotep. My grandfather's names were Amenhotep III, his grandfather's name was Amenhotep II, and his great-grandfather was named Amenhotep I. even my father's original name was Amenhotep IV. It seems as though there was an Amenhotep whom rose to power in every generation, as their where Thutmosis. One or the other would rise to the throne in our dynasty.

Historically, my family is known as the Thutmosides being descendants of Thutmosis I and basically the four Pharaohs that share the same name. My family consisted of two families. The earlier part stemmed from the 17th dynasty beginning with Seqenenre Tao, who was the second to the last, king of the 17th dynasty and ending with Amenhotep I, but recent analogy has unearthed that, that family has been intertwined with another family.

It's not until the infamous Queen Hatshepsut, who some would argue to have been more powerful than Cleopatra IV that the earlier part of the family began to remerge. It is unknown who is the true matriarch or patriarch to the Thumosid line of kings but its suggested that it was a pure blood princess from the earlier part of the family.

The same pattern was repeated but this time when a foreign family, The Mitanni. During the reign of my then grandfather Amenhotep III, the Mitanni, a north eastern civilization became great allies to Egypt. The Mitanni and Egypt exchanged many goods from each other, and one thing that the Mitanni Kings would offer to the King's to Egypt was their daughters.

The first to be sent off was the daughter of the Mittannian king Shuttarna II was Gildukhepa, who was my great aunt and she became my grandfather's secondary wife. It is said that she came with 317 women in waiting. About 15 years later, my mother Tadukhipa was sent to Egypt. History says that the pharaoh fell in love with the princes by the smell of her hair.

My mother's time as my grandfather's concubine came to an end with his death but she swiftly became more than a lesser wife in the eyes of his son Amenhotep IV. In her aunt footsteps she became a secondary wife and dubbed his favorite of all his wives. This is a title that would fuel a war between my mother and the great wife Nefertiti. He jealously was like ticking time bomb just waiting to explode and it soon was.

Out of the love of my two parents came my big sister Tenta'aten (or pronounced Tentenaten). Who were the fourth eldest princes and the first born in my father's city Akhetaten. Lastly, became me Amenhotep "Hung Foot" the youngest of them all. Even though we hail from extremely powerful backgrounds, we were not as important our seven other siblings born to Nefertiti, and one could guess why. But our importance would one day come sadly, but surely.

Only a few years later, and I was already a bouncy healthy toddler. I'm assuming that I was one years old going on two by this time. I've grew up under the care of my mother, her two female attendants, and the careful eye of my father. My father was known as Akhenaten (Akhenaten) another famous 18th dynasty figure whose name meant the "Living spirit of the Aten." Akhenaten was known as the "Heretic Pharaoh" and the world's first monotheist as he set aside the old order of Egyptian Gods and placed the Aten, the sun disk, as the supreme god. This sudden change in religion caused many to hate my father and anyone associated with him, including his children.

My father remained sidelined for the rest of his reign because of his illness, leaving someone else in charge of the kingdom, until my father was cured of his sickness. My father was quite young at the time he looked as if he was about twenty five to twenty-seven years old and very slender. Being so young, I didn't know what was ailing my father so greatly, thus what was happening all around me?

MY LIFE BEFORE

I just knew that he was my father. As I said stated before, my father had a sharp eye on me, due to the fact that I was the youngest of the entire family. My father displayed this as I was amongst other children playing; I was the smallest one in the group amongst me, was two boys' one tall, one short, and a young girl just about my age.

Father watched in delight as we played happily with each other. There was little grass outside it was like we were all like we were all living in the desert. At, first I thought there was no way that people could live in the desert until I learned of the Amarna period in 2010. Could this be the city we were living in? I questioned. It didn't matter to us young ones what we were playing in but we each had fun.

My youthful days were somewhat great times. We always had celebrations in the city. This year, I was going to be part of the parade. The other children and I were given colorful ribbons to wave around the air. I was in the center of my other older siblings, whom held me in a circle, tightly under their protection. As I prance on with my siblings, I saw my father and his chief wife, the beautiful one, also known as Queen Nefertiti (Nefer-tee-tee). My father and his bride both wore marvelous gold and sapphire attire. Nefertiti wore her famous blue cap crown that day, while my father wore the Nemes Headdress, the quite known gold and blue stripped crown that most pharaohs are believed to have worn. "Look Amenhotep!" Nefertiti stated heart felted, "yes!" my father replies proud fully. As I walked past the balcony, where my father and Nefertiti were standing, I couldn't help but noticed that the couple both had sad looks on their face as they were missing someone, someone that they greatly beloved and possibly lost.

Joining us in this parade, were many of our family members. There was our relative Queen Nebetnehat. Nebetnehat's name meant "Lady of the Sycamore Tree." It was unclear who this woman was to me but she was pretty important Lady Nebetnehat had troubled walking on her own.

Slowly, Lady Nebetnehat was being escorted down the long pathway, leading to the main palace by her two trusted female attendants. Nebetnehat wept softly in great pain because of her feet, and walked very slowly behind us. There was something horribly wrong with Lady Nebetnehat's feet that caused her such soreness to walk.

Besides her feet, this woman looked very mature. She looked as if she was within the age group of my father and older than my mother, whom seemed to have looked like she was in her late teens and early twenties at this time. Nebetnehat wore the signature white gown and the golden vulture-winged crown, which meant she was a Great Royal wife. Being a Great Royal Wife meant that Nebetnehat was a chief wife of a Pharaoh, but to whom, I did not know. However, my father had a number of queens. There the famous Queen Nefertiti, and of course my mother. Perhaps, Nebetnehat was a third major queen of my grandfather, or relative of the family. My first suspicions were that she was a very close relative to my father's mother but now I believe she was one of my aunts.

While sneaking along in the shadows of my father's palaces, I've seen many things occur between my royal relatives that no else one has. One time, I watched from afar as my father fidget with his doctors who tried to ease his pain, as though it seemed. The guards struggled to lie my father onto the stone bed my father kept repeatedly whimpered out "no" as the men continued to fight with him. Whatever they were about to do to him might have been very painful

On a bright afternoon, while my mother was chatting with some of the royals a feeling a familiarity came over me as I knew what was going to happen to everyone that was around me. All of the sudden, I blurted out "you all are going to die." Everyone grew quiet when those words muttered from my mouth, but my mother.

"Amenhotep!" mother said appalled at what I said and told me not to say those things. While my mother was putting me in my place, I looked over to see a mysterious boy just glaring at the others then me surprised and possibly scared at what I just said. A part of me feels that he believed in what I said and he was petrified. The boy's stares gave me the chills, even by just remembering the look in his eyes. His stairs were very long and awkward.

It was only a matter of time, and a long time, for me to figure out that this boy was none other than Tutankhamen. Who Tutankhamen was to me, is a mystery. We both lived in the same palace, knew the same people, yet we were worlds apart, separated for unknown reasons, possibly because we came from different backgrounds. I knew little of this boy, and will never get to know him in this former life of my mine. The only thing I can say about him, was from my point of view, he was very quiet and kept to himself a lot.

The first time that I ever heard about King Tut, was when I was about ten or eleven years old. As I recalled it, archaeologists were taking King Tut around the world, or certain places to be presented in museums. His commercials always caught my eyes, as they would show his dazzling gold artifacts and mummy. Something inside of me was saying hmmm, there is something familiar about Tut that drawn my attention to him. A part of me felt like I knew him, and he had some weird connection to me. One late night, while everyone was asleep, I just laid in my bed thinking about him and what his life must have been. Never did it cross my mind that, in a sense, that those feelings that I felt were true. Tut and I were closer than I thought.

It's generally assumed that Tutankhamen and Ankhesenamun (Ankh-seen-amen) was the last of the mighty Thutmoside line. But that assumption is very wrong. Like me, there were others but we all weren't litigable to claim the throne, so our families' ties to the court came to the end but we, as a whole, still remained. Thus the second reason why wanted to write this story, is to tell people that the Thutmoside exist now in the Frazier family line.

Later on, as I was doing my usual strolling around the temples, I've peaked into one of the chambers to see my mother and the shifty Nefertiti standing in front of the balcony chatting amongst each other, their topic was about me. As the memory showed me, Nefertiti was telling my mother that I was too young to have a part in the court, with a deviant smile. I took this as being amongst the royals. From the look of my mother's face she was very upset by Nefertiti's words.

Like my mother, I've grown to have a bitter disliking for Nefertiti. Nefertiti turned out to be really sneaky and snobby at sometimes. One time, while we other children were playing in room, off to where she and her daughters were sitting, one of the boys that I was playing with accidently slipped into the room. The boy was startled when he saw the Nefertiti.

"Shoo!" Nefertiti commanded. "AAAAH!" the boy went off screaming as Nefertiti sat there with her daughters and they laughed at the boy. I stood right in the door way just staring at the Nefertiti furiously. It is also likely that my hatred towards Nefertiti stemmed from the way she treated my mother.

As they say, Nefertiti was a jealous woman, and those of you who said that was right. Nefertiti's hatred towards my mother pushed her to act in the most heinous way. It was late afternoon; my mother and I were tucked in bed. My mother wore a long braided wig, a white gown, and a headband made out of pure solid gold. She lied on her lushes red bed, surrounded by the most pleasant silk curtains that I've ever seen. I laid far side of her in what appeared to be a golden cradle that also had red pillowing like.

As my mother and I slept, my mother found her neck wrapped in the right hand of Nefertiti. Nefertiti was only seconds away from plunging a small knife into my mother, had my mother not grabbed Nefertiti's risk, struggling to hold her back as she held the other risk, as Nefertiti sturdily choked her. The sounds of my mother gagging woke me up. I erupted in tears, seeing my mother trying to defend herself from Nefertiti. As my mother struggled more and more, she the closet thing next to her to get Nefertiti off of her. My mother grabbed the golden candle holder that was sitting next to her bed and struck Nefertiti, hard, several times on the side of the face with the sharp edge of the candle holder.

Finally, Nefertiti then stabs herself on the side with her own blade, as my mother struggled against her. Finally, my mother got up from the bed, with immense strength and struck the Nefertiti hard down to the ground where Nefertiti lied motionless. Blood streamed significantly down from the side of Nefertiti's face. The impact of the candle holder was very crucial. Luckily, the guards came into time. "She tried to kill me!" my mother shouts out to her two guards, still gasping hard to breathe. One of the two guards came down to the floor to check if there was a pulse still within Nefertiti, but there was none, Nefertiti had been slain by my mother.

Shortly after this horrific incident, a huge funeral was held at one of my father's palace for Nefertiti. This small palace was crowded with many servants, family members, and Nobles that were loyal to my father and Nefertiti, who lying in an open casket for all to see. As the guards carried the body of Nefertiti towards the door Ankh, who was young at the time, let out a great cry. Mery stood next to her not muttering a word from her mouth. Ankh and Mery had on these ugly dingy looking brown dresses at the funeral. I assumed that they were playing outside or something, because those were some ugly dresses. Soon after, the guards carried her body out of the opened door never to be seen again.

Nefertiti's hatred for my mother led to her own downfall. She had all the beauty and glory in the world, yet Nefertiti was not satisfied by her exalted status. I guess she wasn't going to allow no one else to take her credibility. Even though she tried to kill my mother, I felt very sympathetic for Nefertiti and almost practically almost moved into tears. It was neither Nefertiti's nor my mother's fault why things were sour between the two of them, it was my father's fault. Perhaps, if my father didn't over looked the other and dubbed one as " The favorite" Nefertiti would still have been alive and Nefertiti's rivalry with my mom wouldn't have been

My grandmother wasn't happy about this. The death of Nefertiti had devastated my grandmother significantly. The fact that my mother killed Nefertiti, cause some serious tension between my grandmother and my mother. I've seen this woman before she would too would often sit and watch us play in the fields. My past grandmother had facial features that resembled that of my present day grandmother. She had the high cheek bones just like her and everything.

A war erupted in the main palace between my mothers, my grandmother, my eldest aunt Sitamun (Seet-amun) (she is not to be confused with my eldest aunt, whom I've mentioned earlier of this life), over the death of Nefertiti. Mother stood alone against the two women, a court full of female attendants, and of course, female family members. Even though there were witnesses, the two guards, to imply the devious deeds of Nefertiti, it was still not enough to woe Grandmother neither Sitamun to believe that my mother was an innocent woman. Grandmother probably assumed that my mother killed Nefertiti out of jealous, which I find very surprising, because it was Nefertiti who was the jealous one, not my mother. First, there was a shouting match between my mother and Sitamun. "You aren't going to marry my brother" Sitamun shouts to my mother implying that she will never take the role as the Chief wife of my father. "No Sitamun" grandmother hushed Sitamun with a wave of her hand, "You will leave this temple" Grandmother Points and shakes her finger at mother. Grandmother was soon going to make sure that he demand was met and my mother be banished from the kingdom.

While my father, grandfather, and the High Priest discussed what to do with my mother, mother impatiently waited in her room for a response, pacing back in forth. My mother paced in her area several times, looking out to the city waiting for a response from my father. My mother wore a white gown that day, but this time with no accessories but she wore her signature wig. Mother looked really concerned and worried about the matter. Meanwhile, I sat in my golden crib just watching her pace back and forth wandering what was wrong with her.

Sadly, just before she could reach the final verdict, it was grandmother's turn to meet her own end as well. On a warm day, Grandmother was laying on a corned bed with her long curly hair flowing out. She looked as if she was very ill because she was sweating intensely. Whatever ailed my grandmother must have been causing her some serious pain. A minute later, grandmother calls out the name of a person named Nebetah.

"Nebetah! Nebetah!" My grandmother slowly called out with her eyes closed. Grandmother's voice was so deep or hard as one would say but she looked so surprised at the same time.

This mysterious person, that she called out for was not inside the room when grandmother was calling out her name. Shortly after, the room grew silent and grandmother had passed.

Nebetah, who name means "Lady of the Palace", was one of six, or eight daughters of Amenhotep III and Queen Tiye, who can now be identified as my then grandmother. Nebetah was also thought to be the mother of Tutankhamen by some archaeologist, and this assumption is indeed true, but that's not all. The shy young princess may have been Queen Nefertiti herself. Nebetah may have changed her name to Neferneferuaten to support her brothers Aten religion and the name Nefertiti was part of that. Nebetah was the only one of my aunts that didn't get married to my then grandfather, other than the youngest Beketaten.

Nebetah was the next in line to become queen and seeming how grandfather was dead, grandmother must have married her two children together. At last, the mighty Queen reunited with her beloved daughter on the other side. My grandmother died within her early to mid-50s which suggest that my father had to have been in his mid to late 20s to early 30s when she died.

Queen Tiye's characteristics remind me so much of my present day grandmother's characteristics. Like my present day grandmother, Tiye was very caring, and formidable. She was very much involved in her children's life. Both are matriarch of our family, the sun that shined on, we, her descendants. If my present grandmother were to go out, then our world would be dismantled, because she is the glue that holds everything together.

In this life, my mother and grandmother don't get along. It is mostly because of my mother. I never understand why mother held such a strong grudge against her own mother. My grandmother and I didn't get along either, but to hold a grudge, it not my thing. I'm a type a person who would get angry, but if you give me a while, I'll get over it. Really, I just get irritated to easily, and I've been told many times that I need to work on that. I'm also a forgiving person. It was my mother herself, who taught me to forgive people, no matter how awful the situations might have been. But, she herself, never master this hard lesson.

My mother always felt as if she was different from her sisters and brothers, and I now know why. Originally, she didn't start up in this family and she was once a foe to Queen Tiye. When we die and reincarnate old family members and friends still remain close in their own ways.

"So that's where it all started" I joked to myself, implying about my mother's feud against my grandmother. I seriously, wish that the two of them, and everyone else that are feuding would settle their differences. Mother if you are reading this, once you forgive, you heal. This is something that I wish you grasp in the future.

Interestingly, the Amarna family shared a lot of things in common with my modern family. For example, Queen Tiye has almost the same amount of children as my present day grandmother. My grandmother has two boys and four girls whereas Queen Tiye had two boys and four girls that is if two of them are the same person. Another thing is our facial features. Majority of my great aunts including my grandmother have this strong feature in this face. Another notable feature is the large incisor. Nearly everyone in our family has bucked teeth and majority of them are gapped. It is always amusing to me how much in common my present family has with the late 18th dynasty pharaohs. Heck, I even thought that we were somehow related to them via through mitochondrial DNA, meaning from my mother side of the family. My reasons why I believed this? Well you have to keep reading to find out.

Queen Tiye is one of my most favorite Queens in the entire ancient world. To me, Queen Tiye, was the most powerful Queen in ancient history due to how much power she had in her husband's reign. No other woman in that time frame ever rivaled such power and it took Centuries later for woman to actually stand up and be that independent. In my opinion, Queen Tiye is a prime example of a strong woman and I'm influenced by her strength, power, and dedication to her husband and children these are acts I intend to follow. I applaud Queen Tiye for being such a powerhouse, all hail the queen.

It was training day for Tutankhaten. Tutankhamen was being trained to be a warrior. Tut was a bit older than myself, perhaps five or six years apart from each other. I've sat and watched Tut train with his trainer under an opened shelter decorated with pink and yellow draperies that hang from this shelter.

MY LIFE BEFORE

Tut and the young man, whom looked about half of Tutankhamen's age, were dressed in blue and god attire. More like a sapphire battle armor with the golden wings of a bird (or eagle) crossing over its surface. The young man wore the blue Khepresh Crown, so his status was very high here in our city. He may have been my father's co-regent, who name was Smenkhare (Smenkar-re) Smenkhare's name meant "Living is the forms of Ra." Young Tutankhamen was being trained how to battle, in case he would have to go into war someday, when he would become king. Tut bested Smenkhare in this training session knocking Smenkhare to his feet. The two were really enjoying themselves that day. Except for me, who had couldn't participate due to being the smallest in the area. This would be the last time that I would see my father's co-regent. It was completely unknown to me, as to what happened to Smenkhare.

Shortly, after the death of Nefertiti it was time to crown the next heir of the throne, and as you all know, that the next heir to throne was Tutankhaten. The future boy king was being escorted by guards (by hand) to where ever the guards were taking him, perhaps another part of the palace. As Tut and the guards were walking by, tut glared at me and I noticed the worried look on his face. He might have been worried as to what was about to happen to him

Like I mentioned earlier, Tut was very shadowy to me even in that time, I knew little of him, and what was going on in this time period. But, when I did my research and looked back on this memory, I realized that he was afraid, afraid of becoming the next king of Egypt. Judging from all that took place in our home, I could see why. The worried Tut stood looking over the stone banister one day staring into the unknown. Tut seemed very withdrawn from everyone most of the time, almost as if he was in another world or something. We, other young royals, had more free will than Tut. He would always be off to himself while we other children would go out and play

As I ran through the temple, trying to get out of the rain, I heard someone crying, so I went to go see who it was that sounded so sad. It was none other than Tutankhaten. "Why are you crying?" I asked him "I don't to be Pharaoh" Tut cried. I told him to stop crying and that being a Pharaoh is a great thing. I've talked to Tut for a very brief a moment. I yelled at him telling him to stop crying and to get him to cheer up. It rained upon us as we talked but our talked came to a quick end as the guards came to snatch the Tut up. They literally snatched him up too. That was the last time that I saw Tutankhaten ever again.

On my last walk around the palace, I saw my father's sickness for my own eyes, and it wasn't a pretty sight. As I entered the room where he was resting, I gazed upon My father's eye's he looked horrible one of his eyes were a different color than the other and his face looked as if he was some sort of ugly monster this horrified me but, it pained him as he called out my name repeatedly and I didn't respond I hid behind the wall connected to his room nodding my head no as father kept calling out my name. This made him sob intensively.

That day came when my father had to decide what he was going do with my mother. My mother stood with her head held high, probably thinking that my father wouldn't do the unthinkable to her because she was his beloved, but unfortunately, love didn't play a part in this gathering. The verdict has been reached for my mother. My father had decided to banish my mother from the kingdom she was never to return again, but my mother wasn't going to leave alone. My mother strongly fussed to take me or my full older sister Tenta'aten, or Tentenaten with her. Father only allowed mother to take only one of us.

"Go" my father waved his hands, signaling my mother to leave the Kingdom at once. My father had on his signature outfit sitting on his throne with a golden cane drenched in real gold and golden cape, and wearing a golden featured crown. From this moment on, I never saw my father, Tut, Tenta'aten, and the rest of my family again

The next thing I knew, after that day, my mother and I were being taken to live north east of Amarna. I awoke in the carriage to see my mother sitting on the far side of me looking out of the window of the carriage very sad. "Take me from this place." My mother commanded the carriage driver. So off we went into the unknown. I assumed that we rode off before anyone woke up to notice that we were all gone. I could remember being in a carriage and looking up to the dim sky as we rode off there was no one insight as we made our departure. As I looked up into the sky, I noticed how close the sides of the large buildings were. They were relatively close to each other and perfectly straight, there was another us carriage next to us and both carriages were riding off at dawn to where ever we were going. It was unknown as to who was in the carriage beside us, but it was likely that it was my mother's trusted guards who were banished along with us.

After my mother and I's departure, we had a hard time coping with what was to be our new lifestyle. I remember when it was pouring down raining my mother had us sitting in was to me some sort of cave. She had me bundled up in her lap under her black cloak you wouldn't know if I was under there because I was so tiny. While my mother sat there sadly I fundled with her giant golden knecklace. My mother was identical to a solar sytem, you know the ring the planets made around the sun. However, this giant knecklace has three golden balls on it that were line up with each other, a very weird piece of jewerly I might add.

Several times I played with it the large ring. "stop it, stop it Amenhotep!" my mother commanded and I obeyed. Being only a infant, I didn't know why mother was so sad and the reason for us being where we were, but I always will remember the sad look on my mother's face that day.

"I will never forget what he done to me" my mother would muttered, each time my mother would talk about her past in Egypt. Its unfortunate that my mother never healed from her banishment away from Egypt, but I could tell that the love for my father was still very alive inside my mother but the pain overceed it each time.

Awaiting our arrival at my mother's old home, were these two men, who I believe were my uncles and my mother's mother, Queen Juni the widow of King Tushratta, the former ruler of Mitanni. These people were very happy to see us when we arrived, especially My Grandmother. As soon as my grandmother saw me, she instantly fell in love with me, reaching her arms out to grasp me as my mother and I walked me towards her. I was very surprised, as I didn't know whom these people were in front of me. Grandmother Juni was an old women with grey hair that almost appeared to be white and she was also a very sweet woman. From this time on, my mother and I would be living under the protection of her two guards and her mother.

MEETING PHAROAH SETI I

Some years have passed, and I was now fully grown. I've been living with my mother for quite a while. My mother was still very beautiful and almost as if she hadn't aged a bit since I was an infant. My own appearance was quite stunning as well. In an odd way, I looked similar to a female, even though I was very much a male. My head was shaven, and I had wide hips, just like most females. For a male, I had a very decent appearance just as remarkable as my mother's appearance.

Easily, I could have been passed as a female to most people back then. I don't know why I had a female appearance in my past life; it's a mystery that still puzzles me to this day. From the time that these memories began, my original assumption was that I was just a female in that life, thus I only recognized myself as a man (meaning how I am today). It was really confusing to tell which sex I was.

Before I learned of Akhenaten, and the other late 18th dynasty household names, my other assumption was that I was a beautiful hermaphrodite in my past life, because I literally looked like a woman. That's when I learned of Akhenaten having to have wide hips and feminine appearance like I did. My jaw dropped yet again and it didn't take long for me to put two and two together, suggesting I was from the same bloodline.

After all that happened to us, I became my mother's biggest concern. My mother knew very well what was going on in Egypt, as she apparently was keeping in contact with my sisters. It must have bothered her dearly that I wasn't doing anything important, or involved with my other royal family back in Egypt. One day, she rode into town in a carriage draped with black curtains. My mother halted the carriage when she saw me at the market place talking to some guy. He was well muscled and very attractive. It shocked my mother when she saw us hugged up as if we were in love, which we really were. She looked away slowly in concern. Right there and then, I believe my mother made up her mind as what she wanted to do with me.

One day, Mother called upon me to her nicely tented throne, covered around with the finest white silk. Mother also wore the finest jewelry that I've ever seen. My mother still had that sad look her face and she told me "to go to Egypt". It was my understanding that my mother wanted me to go live with my sisters, whom at which, neither of us have seen in years. At this point, it was very elusive to me as to what happened to my family after my mother and I departed from Egypt, a decade ago. I just knew bits and pieces of what went on over that past few years since our departure. So off I went, to my birthplace in Egypt.

Upon my arrival to my sister's house, my two eldest sisters, Ankh and Mery, were very excited to see me when I arrived, as it was a very long time since we all seen each other. At this time, there was only a few of my relatives still living in Egypt, and I had no clue what had happened to the rest of my family.

My Eldest sister was named Meritaten, but we called her Mery for short. Meritaten meant *"She who is beloved by the Aten."* Mery was a devoted follower of the Aten just like our father and her mother. Mery was now the matriarch of our now dwindled family. Mery always kept a keen eye on us and look out for us very well. Mery stayed off to herself a lot, in a way, it seems she was trying to stay out of harm's way. Mery lurked in the shadows of me and Ankh. Despite, how she felt about the royals of that time. However, she remained very loyal to them possibly fearing what they could do to her, as she have seen many things than, we, her younger siblings have.

Even though Mery was the head of the family, my middle sister, Ankh was the heart of our family. Ankh's spirit lit up the room. Ankh's full name was Ankhesenpa'aten (Ankh-en-se-pa-aten), which mean, *"Her life is the Aten."* But many people assume she is Queen Ankhesenamun (Ankh-e-sen-amun) which means *"Her life is Amun"*, the sister-wife of King Tutankhamen. Personally, I believe that this is just simply a mistake in identity and Ankhesenamun in which everyone spoke of is of someone who once shared a similar named, a princess called Ankhesenpa'aten Tasherit. Like my sister Mery, my sister's name was abbreviated and we called her Ankh for short

Ankh and Mery were very close and were within the same age group. She was the most open one, meaning that she was the one that reported first to Seti, the one he talked to the most. As soon as I got to Egypt, Ankh and I immediately began to get close. In fact, I was closer to Ankh than my other three sisters. I didn't get to know my two sisters that well, as I departed from them before I got the chance to. However, now that we were reunited, I was about to make up for lost time.

Interestingly enough, I was never around my sisters when I was a toddler. We never even played with each other around the temple, like that other children did nor did we even associate with each other. It was like we all co-existed where we once lived but my sisters obviously knew of me quite well to want me to come live with them. The way my sisters were living wasn't lavish but peasant like; but decent enough to live I can say for the least. They lived in this brown, mud or brick house amongst other civilians that were considered low class citizens. This place was to be my home for the next few years.

Tenta'aten (Ten-ta-aten) her name reads *"She of the Aten"* was there with Ankh and Mery as well. Tenta'aten now had some strong resemblance to our mother. You might say she was the spitting image of her. In complexion, Tenta'aten was darker than me and my other three sisters and one of the quietest persons in the house. Tenta'aten and I never interacted for some strange reasons. We both lived in the same house, yet we hardly spoke. It was like we both lived in a different world from each other, a world I wasn't allowed to enter. A part of me feels that she was angry at me because our mother left her in Egypt. Being left behind like, that must have devastated Tenta'aten especially what was to come after our departure. Sadly, we will never be able to resolve this issue.

My fourth sister, Setepenre (pronounced Sote-pen-re) whose name meant *"Chosen of Re"* Setepenre was the youngest of my three older sisters, and of all my sisters. She would always stay close behind Mery and Ankh and hardly said a word. Setepenre was not that much older than myself. In fact, we were in the same age group. Likewise, Tenta'aten and Setepenre were ever hardly around most of the time, but Setepenre was around more than Tenta'aten and I think that's likely because Tenta'aten did not want to be anywhere around me. Setepenre would sometimes mutter quietly to herself, but it didn't bother us at all.

My four older sisters were fairly beautiful woman but their lives were very complicated, and it was because of our father. He and Nefertiti had no idea that their beloved children would one day end up being peasants. Father's vision was a dreadful nightmare for us all as it caused my sisters and me great troubles for years to come.

All of my sisters worked for the new royals in their palace. Mery and Ankh were the royals' main female servants, as the two of them handled important matters for Seti and possibly even his wife, Tuya. I don't know how long they were working for the royal couple but I've been shown something that may have led to them working for Seti and it probably from what I've been told from each of my sisters.

In this memory, possibly given to me from the stories told from my sisters, Mery was cast aside when Ankh and Tutankhamen became the next King and Queen of Egypt after our father's passing. Although I'm not sure I believe that Ankh was just playing as the infamous Queen Ankhkheperure-Nefernefertaten who served as Tut's co-gerent for the first two years and a month of Tut's reign. Alone, Mery fought hard to keep our father's values and name alive, she wasn't about to let everything that our father created go down into flames. No one wanted the Aten cult, the cult in which my father worshipped the sun disk, therefore a single god, to press on much further. Mery was trying to press our father's religion further.

Sadly, Mery lost the battle against the High priest of Amun and was disgraced along with Tentenaten and Setepenre.

Mery was devastated when the Priest banished her away from the court, the palace, more so her own siblings. Heavily, Mery begged to Ankh, pleading to Ankh and Tut so that they could change their minds, but there was nothing Ankh could do. Ankh and Tut stood on their thrones, looking away from Mery, as if she was nothing. Mery broke into tears, groveling on the floor, but her tears weren't enough to change their minds. For that particular moment, that was the last time Ankh would see Mery, Setepenre, and Tenta'aten. Ankh and Tut were being heavily manipulated by the High priest and probably acted that way out of fear and persuasion. Deep down inside, Ankh didn't want to do what she did to her sisters and probably felt that that Mery had betrayed Tut in some for. I'm not sure what exactly went on to cause Ankh to act like this towards Mery but it had to have been something very serious.

As a result of their disgrace; Mery, Tentenaten, and Setepenre all found themselves living amongst Commoners, people whom used to serve them, distant away from where Ankh, Ankhesenamun and Tutankhamen were staying. But, it was not long for Ankh to find herself joining her other sisters in their disgrace. She too was soon about to meet her fate and her reign was coming to an end.

One dark night, while everyone in the area was asleep; Ankh came banging on Mery's door, crying on her knees. Ankh had on lavish gold, a nice white gown, and the Great Royal Wife Crown.

"I'm sorry" Ankh cried deeply and softly to Mery for what she done to her a while back. Being forgiving and sympathetic for her younger sister, Mery helped Ankh off the ground and slowly walked Ankh into the house. Thus, Ankh joined; Mery, Tenta'aten, and Setepenre in their peasant like life. Ankh had a hardest time coping with her new lifestyle but Mery was always there to comfort her.

One day, (as it was shown to me) my sisters were sitting amongst other peasants, or homeless people eating bread. Everyone but Ankh was eating bread. Ankh sat beside Mery looking very sad. Mery looked to her sister and said "everything is going to be alright", attempting to cheer Ankh up. Sadly, what Mery told Ankh was far from the truth. As I said before, my sisters' lives were all pretty complicated before my mother and I departed from Egypt and was doomed for the same pattern, and I was to join them in their life of misery. I just added a twist to their story.

Immediately, as I got out my carriage, I was to report to Seti's palace. Mery and Ankh assisted me in getting myself prepared to become a household male servant to Prince Seti. We were to have a meeting with Seti himself. My sisters straightened me up and rubbed me down with oil. I was shirtless and wore a golden necklace around my neck and a white cloth around my lower waistline. Mery gave me my father's golden wristband with Sapphire jewels on it. My father once wore this beautiful jewelry on his arm, and it was left to me as a gift before he died my sisters Mery seemed to have treasured it ever since.

Mery kept some of her belongings, as well as, many of our deceased relative's belongings in a black chest. This black chest sat in the back of the house, cloaked by the shadows of the house. Mery's black chest is where she also pulled this golden armband from.

This golden armband was very precious to me. I wore this golden wristband on my right arm. Even in this life, I could even feel it on me, even though I do not have it on me today. Weird isn't it, I always felt like something was missing on my right arm, like I've lost something that I used to have on it once upon a time. Now I know where that sensation came from. Once Mery and Ankh were finished with me, my sisters gave me some tips on how to behave in front of Seti and his court. I wasn't too keen about behaving right for someone that I thought wasn't very important to me, or someone that thought they were better than me. I'm still very much like this; I don't take no mess out of no man or woman. In this life, I was a rebel in my own way. But for the sake of myself, and my sisters, I had to change my attitude a bit in order to get this job.

Just as Mery and Ankh were doing some finishing touches on me, Setepenre comes into our home unannounced. Setepenre was also prince Seti's female messenger. She would out and deliver messages for the young prince. For this reason she was hardly around.

Despite her task as being a messenger, Setepenre always stood behind Mery and Ankh whenever they would go before Seti or there was an important meeting to attend held by the king. Mery and Ankh did most of the talking, practically of all the servants. Seti had a great deal of trust in my two eldest sisters and I think it was because of their royal background.

"Seti had sent for you" Setepenre tells us. Quickly, Ankh and Mery did some little finishing touches on me before we could go off to the temple. I had to look my best as first impressions even mattered to Seti from all his servants. So, the four of us went off to the Seti's Palace. My sisters and I lived outside the royal palace it was a long walk to get to the Seti's palace. Our house was on the far left, close to the village's opening. Seti's palace stood very tall in fact; it was the biggest thing in the entire area. There was this huge black statue that stood before Seti's palace. This statue was huge and black and stood right outside the balcony bedroom. The statue looked as if it was a four legged creature sitting with its front paws out also wearing a Nubian style wig. I couldn't make out exactly what the creature was but it was a strange looking statue.

When we all arrived to the palace, immediately we went to the main room where Seti was awaiting for us. I was so nervous about meeting Seti. As soon as I got there, all eyes were on me. Everyone one, the nobles and other associates of Seti looked at me up and down and were whispering to their friends about me, about how I looked. One guy looked very surprised to see me as if he knew who I was or something. I could hear them snickering and laughing, but I didn't mind it at all, only just a little bit.

Slowly, I approached Seti who was sitting on his throne alongside his wife to be, Mut-Tuya (pronounced Moot-Tooya). Lady Tuya was very short but a very beautiful woman. Seti himself looked very remarkable. Seti had a nicely chiseled dark chest, nice abs, and handsome smooth face. Around his neck, Seti always wore this beautiful sapphire beetle around his neck. It was absolutely the most gorgeous piece of jewelry that I've ever seen in my entire life. Seti sat there laid back with his beautiful dark muscles just waiting for me to enter room, well not exactly; he looked a little bored to me and uninterested in my service at all. Seti had an unpleased look on his face which scared me and I didn't think I would get the job. Mery and Ankh tried introduced me to the Seti, thus tried to tell the young prince about me, but Seti silenced them making Tuya smirk.

Despite all I said about Queen Tuya, she was very spoiled and literally enjoyed her status as Seti's wife. Tuya quickly gained my bitter envy. Lady Tuya was my rival in the palace. She would hate my guts, and I would soon hate hers.

"What is your name?" Prince Seti asked,

"Amenhotep" I responded tenderly and nervously shaking from where I stood.

"The son of Neferkheperure (pronounced Nefer-khepre-Ure) Waenre and Tadukhipa-Kiya" I implied," but, everyone calls me Hung Foot", I responded.

Hung Foot is the name that I'm called almost throughout memories. I assumed that this was my real name, but since the Amarna memories, I know that it is not. Why I was called this was unknown, and who gave me this nickname. Perhaps, it was because it appeared to others that I had a hanging foot.

However, a notable feature that I share in this life was that I always stood with one feet resting on the other. I never knew where this weird habit started I guess it began in my past life from standing in Seti's temple all the time.

Seti then asked me what my age was. I'm nineteen years old" I told Seti.

Seti then questioned me about my past and what I am capable of doing, and then he mocked me by saying this rude remark

"Are you going to bring back the Aten?" Seti teased, smiling at me. Seti made the people in his throne room laugh. But I wasn't about to take that especially from no royal doochebag

"If you tempt me enough then I would" I sassed and smiled back at him. Almost instantly, the room grew silent when those words came out of my mouth. Not a single word everyone was quiet for a brief moment.

Startled by my reaction to Seti's remarks, Ankh and Mery both looked up to the Seti, fearful to see what he was about to do to me.

Astonishingly, Seti laughs it off and then hired me for the job thus making me his newest servant. He-he what a big relief he might have gave my sisters. I didn't know it then, but I think this was the start of something really ugly; I had sparked Seti's interest.

Therefore because of that, I think that's why I got the job as a palace servant unlike my four sisters. My sisters were not mere house servants like myself. My sisters had more important duties around the palace pacifically Mery and Ankh. The two of them would help Seti with foreign affairs and even with situations within Egypt itself. On one occasion, while Seti was away, the young king to be allowed my sister Ankh to run things. Ankh sat writing a on a beige piece of paper leaning on the right arm of Seti's throne (Ankh was right handed by the way). Mery stood on the right next to her while my other two sisters stood behind the throne. Apparently my sisters were pretty good at what they were doing for Seti to have allowed them to take care of things while he was away.

That day, I instantly began work inside the palace. My sister's high positions kept us apart in the palace. I hardly even saw them except when we went back home, and when there was something important going on in Seti's throne room. It was like we each lived a different life once we hit the palace doors. My first task was serving food to the royal family. The other men at Seti's table at like savages. Their manners were completely disgusting I frowned in disgust as I watched them eat. As we servants, sat food down on their table the people sitting there would mock us and make fun of us.

The men's remarks made us felt bad and at the same time very angry. All but one man ate and that man was Seti. As I set down the bowl on the table I just so happened to look up noticed Seti glaring at me and smiling. Quickly as I could, I looked down to the ground not wanting to show the slightest emotion in front of Seti, because I was still very humiliated by his friends at the table. Again, Seti was shirtless and he wore his favorite sleek sapphire beetle necklace. Seti's grin was so cute, what an incredible looking man God had before Seti always had his eyes on me which puzzled me. His glares would always send chills down my spine.

MY LIFE BEFORE

The Royals had a lack of respect for us servants especially for me and everyone that were lower than them. One evening Seti was chatting with Tuya and Queen Sitre, Seti's mother. As ordered I was sent to bring Seti a cup of wine. The drink was sitting in a gold cup thus sitting on a gold plate which I was holding in my palms. As I approached Seti, he slapped me hard in the face knocking the cup out of my hand. Seti fussed "I don't want this". Angry and eager to do something to Seti, I slowly turned my head towards Seti to find his wife and mother glaring angrily angry at me. Knowing that I couldn't, I slowly turned my head to Seti to find him and the woman giving me stern stares. All I could do is clean up the mess and walk away from them. The whole ordeal was sabotage someone was setting me up for failure someone which I never caught in his or her act.

Very unpleased by my performance around the palace or just frustrated by my presence, Seti wanted to get rid of me. I remember Seti leaning over on his throne wearing a white garment pointing his finger at me saying" "I should send you back to Mitanni", the place where I lived before I came back to Thebes. Seti argued with his mother, Queen Sitre to send me back home. Upon standing afar, with my sisters waiting on Seti's final decision, Mery told me "that is going to be alright" trying to comfort me. However, the situation didn't bother me at all. Sending me back, would've probably been the best thing Seti has ever done for me at that moment. But, much to my dismay, Queen Sitre was on my side and was able to change her son's mind giving me the chance to stay with my sisters.

Queen Sitre (also known as Tia-Sitre) was the Great Royal Wife of Ramses I, the father of Seti the first, and the grandfather of Ramses the Great. Queen Sitre's name meant "Daughter of Ra, another apparition the Egyptian sun god, Amun-ra. Everyone, including myself, adored the queen, so much so that it got on her nerves (Giggles), I remember everyone was calling out her name trying to get her attention and she responded irritated with a "what?" I felted so embarrassed when she yelled at us, but Seti laughed. God I hated that man. Sitre was a very beautiful woman and very powerful might I add, but you want to know what else was very surprising. Seti's mother was Angela Basset, a famous actress best known for her roles in Waiting to Exhale and "How Stella got her Groove Back" and much more.

Freaky isn't it? It was surprising to me when she appeared in my first premonitions." I knew Angela Basset once upon a time?" I thought to myself. Man, I was so scared to even right this part in my book because I was too afraid that Mrs. Basset would call up her agent to come get me and kick my ass or would be waiting to exhale some fire under me but then I thought, it wouldn't hurt, right? The writing part I meant.

Queen Sitre was very admired by many, mostly women and I just as well as I admire Angela Basset in my current life. Angela always has such a great and very strong performance when she performs in movies. Angela makes you feel exactly whatever she going through in that movie. What I found ironic was that Seti looked exactly how Angela's love interest looked in "How Stella Got Her Groove Back". Oh god I'm getting heated just talking about him (Stella's man), what a good movie that was.

If it was one queen to have met from the ancient times it would've been Queen Tia-Sitre. Queen Sitre always appeared to be calm and humble just like her son, I could see where Seti got his nice demeanor from, he got it from his mother. Sometimes the queen would hardly speak a word just observe especially when her husband was around. Despite being a non-popular queen in Egyptology, Queen Sitre is actually my number one favorite Queen in ancient Egyptian history due to my personal acquaintance with the queen. She was such a great person to have known.

Initially, I used to have the assumption that Tia-Sitre was identical to Ankhesenpaaten's wet nurse Tia and therefore the reason why my sisters and I were able to work amongst the palace with her husband and son. I always wondered if my memories were true, then how we even survived, seeming that our father was the most hated pharaoh in all Egypt. Presumably, I thought I got my answer. It's no wonder why I like her so much in that life, she was dear to our family we owe her our lives for practically spearing them, heck she owed us because if it wasn't for the connection to Ankh, she probably wouldn't been in the position she was in. a part of me feels like Tia's ties to our family was a lot closer than one originally thought.

As for Seti's father, I've ran into him in various occasions, I never really interact with Seti's father, Ramses I, as I was assigned a servant of his son. So I never really got a chance to get to know the first Ramses however we did encounter. One evening Seti and his mother were assisting a withering Ramses onto his golden chair. Ramses looked as if he was sick I assume the king was slowly dying from something that's when I came into the room and at the moment the elderly Ramses muttered some harsh words. Ramses stated "get this scourge of Amarna out of his sight" those words hurt my feelings greatly and I could see that Seti saw the hurt on my face.

Despite the fact that I was disliked by Seti's father, it appears that I've become a popular figure around the palace. Everyone in the palace knew me and became people that I was well associated with. While I was busy chatting with other servants of the palace, laughing and enjoying the conversation that we were having, Seti stood afar with one of his priest observing me.

"Who is this slave?" An old priest asked Seti. "Amenhotep" thus continued to observe me.

I guess my presence in the palace sparked a flame in the room or something, because despite my treatment from the upper classmen and the royals, I was sort of a celebrity around town. I think this is why the old fellow asked who I was. The royals and High Priest probably wondered why this mere servant was gaining so much attention. Maybe it was my personality or cute feminine charms. Another plausible reason because I was of the former ruling house. I was technically related to nearly almost every Pharaoh that has gone before Seti I. Thus from a family who ruled Egypt for centuries within two dynasties. Who knows, but was I getting along with almost everyone. Imagine that a servant gaining all the attention from the royals. I must have been some talker back then.

I gained a new best friend. She was (and still is) a close friend we would always laugh and joke about things that we found funny or weird. One time, we servants were standing behind Seti and the other royals who were watching the slaves built up his monuments. My new friend and I were laughing and giggling behind their backs.

Unexpectedly, I didn't notice until later on that Seti was staring at me. It startled me to see him staring at me I thought I was going to get in trouble or something I stopped laughing when he turned around and looked at me. Then he turned around and said something to his wife and friends that made them chuckle. I don't know what he said but I knew it was about us. Then my friend said something else about them that made me giggled.

My friend and I always made jokes of Seti and everyone else behind Seti's back. One time, during some royal arrangement me and my friend stood far from the throne and my friend pointed out that Seti's head was partially shaven. I tried so hard not to laugh but eventually I did and loud too. My loud laughter caught everyone's attention. Seti asks me "What's so funny Amenhotep?" I shook my head, implying that nothing was funny, lying being afraid that I was going to get in trouble. Seti looked so funny with his head half chopped that night, it was so funny.

As the days went by, I even began to work now for Lady Tuya, much to my dismay. Lady Tuya was such a spoiled woman; she literally got everything she wanted and if she didn't, she would have it fit. One day, the guards were carrying on some flat thing. My guard lover purposely made Tuya fall off the thing. Tuya rolled down the steps like a boiling ball. Everyone, especially me, laughed I guess it was Tuya's bad karma finally kicking in.

One early morning, while we were at the temple, I noticed a strange woman in a black cloak going about her business. It appears that the woman was hiding herself from everyone under that cloak. It appears that Seti's guards knew this woman and poked fun at her. The vile guards walks towards her and tried to pull the black cloak off of her. The sickly woman helplessly tried to tug away from them. Finally, the guards were able to pull off the black cloak thus revealing the faces underneath the cloak. To our surprise, the woman's entire body was covered with bumps that looked like she had measles or the chicken pox. These bumps were huge. The woman appeared to have been suffering from a severe skin disease.

MY LIFE BEFORE

As the woman cried out for help, her voice was faint and hag like. Horrified the woman cried out "Help me!" and as she approached a guard for help another comes behind her and hit her in the head with a rock therefore knocking her down to the ground. My two sisters immediately ran to help the mysterious woman. "Beke!" they called out to this woman. Ankh and Mery were both overwhelmed of grief as the woman lie there motionless. Ankh held the woman's head in her hands and cries out "why" and let out a great cry. I never have seen Mery and Ankh so emotional like that my entire time living with them.

Apparently, the mysterious woman was a close relative of ours. The woman spent most of her days hiding herself in her cloak and in our home in fear of the cruelty of the outside world. My sisters, my middle sister especially, took good care of her and she was known to them as Beke. I, like so many others disliked Beke due to her sickly appearance. It bothered me sometimes to even look at her especially when she would scratch her skin to me it was difficult to watch.

The memory of this mysterious woman came to me, in a vision, one day while I was digging for information on both; Meritaten and Ankhesenamun, the daughters of Akhenaten and Nefertiti, whom I believed where my two sisters Mery and Ankh, but had their names shortened. I kept thinking about how harsh life had to been for them after all their father have done to Egypt and this vision came. The name of the woman stuck out to me the most, Beke. I immediately assumed that the identity of this woman was known other than Princess Beketaten, the youngest daughter of Queen Tiye and Amenhotep III, thus one of my father's sisters making Beke one of my aunts. With this memory, I was more than convinced that I was once a relative to the Amarna Dynasty.

Seti's rude guards and troops always have a nasty way of toying with people. One dark night, prince Seti and his troops came home celebrate one of their victories over the north eastern civilizations in which they fought in a war. Seti looked marvelous in his gold plated armor with his shiny war helmet. We servants were already lined up to serve him and his fellow troops

Before the celebration, Seti gave a great speech to his soldiers, and then he sat in his chair with his whine cup in his right hand. Seti lifts up in gratitude just before everyone began to celebrate. That night the troops drank and party like wild animals. It was a thrilling and exciting to see everyone dance. But, some of the warriors weren't as pleasant to get along with as they were rude and some were very mild-mannered towards some of us but they were mostly drunk and having a good time. One of the warriors thought it would be cool to scare me so he came up to me and screamed in my face.

"Blaaah!" this ignorant fool screamed causing me to shake in my boots and piss my loins. The warrior and several warriors laughed at me making me feel very humiliated.

This was not the end of my torture some stupid hoodlums threated to inflict harm on me and chased me all the way home. For reasons why, I did not knew, but I suspect that because I was the spawn of the heretic pharaoh that everyone have come to hate. Surprisingly, as I made it to the front door the men were not behind me. Perhaps Seti stopped the men from bothering me because after this no one picked on me again.

Seti's right hand man, his leading lieutenant and most of everyone that was there, were all people whom I've had the pleasure of meeting in this life. I use to find this too fantasy like, but I soon discover that this could've been possible. We may have already known that person from another lifetime. Of course, they didn't look like that; I guess it was me recognizing their souls.

Majority of everyone that worked for Seti, were people that I've stumbled across in my present life. All this time we would talk to each other and pass each other, little did we know that we all have already met. I believe my life in Egypt may have been the first time I may became acquainted with these persons. One time, I was watching a segment with Silvia Browne on YouTube Silvia stated "That everyone that we meet in Heaven our people that we already encounter in another life time". Now I'm not one of those peoples to get in to all the psychic stuff, but when Silvia said this, I was questioning the possibility as of how? Is this even true but I've come to learn that there is a possibility

I've learned a lot from Silvia Browne about past lives and spirituality. Even though most people would argue that Silvia isn't a legible psychic, I really didn't care about that stuff, because for the most part, I was seeking answers only she and a few others have answered. A lesson that I've earned from Silvia is when you do something to someone that is bad and you don't get your dish of Karma, you are likely to get it in the next life (Silvia Browne). So now I'm more careful at what I do to people, even though some people do deserve an ass or two to kiss.

Silvia's life lessons of spirituality has opened my eyes, and warped my mind from the arrogant and close-minded teachings that I was taught throughout my present lifetime, so there, I give the woman some props. I too think that if one has a strong spirituality, he or she will be able to identify themselves more and have a strong will for themselves.

There was a dance in the palace at sun set. Everyone, including my sisters and I wore white gowns and looked our finest. Everyone spun around with their dance partners to the music. I was asked to dance by my sister Ankh. "Dance with me Amenhotep" Ankh asks, and so I did. Ankh spun around joyously as I held her hand having a good time. My other sisters were enjoying themselves as well.

While my Tenta'aten and Setepenre danced together, Mery clapped her hands to the beat of the music smiling and laughing. This was a very exciting dance for all of us. It was an especially great moment to see my sisters enjoying themselves for a chance. God knew that they needed to so.

LOVE ONE'S LOST

On a gloomy night, Seti and Tuya were getting intimidate, you know, doing the do. I along with several other servants, were standing in the room as the prince and his wife was about to do it the other guards started to touch themselves I didn't know what to do so I followed the king saw this and smiled but the queen ordered us out of the room.

"Out", Tuya lifted her finger. I didn't know what I doing, I just thought it was something we were supposed to do but anyways it was the most embarrassing thing I've ever done. This incident was so uncomfortable that I didn't even want to put it inside this book. Just thinking about it sends an embarrassing chill down my spine. However, it shined some light on my gender identity; I was a man, a man with some very girlish features.

As time went on, I've become even more accustom to the lifestyle as a household servant. Majority of the time, me and some other servants would dance with some on the guards. I danced on my upon my lover's groan making him blush with excitement, and everyone shouting exciting at what I just did. Dancing was my signature thing back then, the way I moved was like a belly dancer. I was a good dancer the guards enjoyed it including the King.

Seti walked passed up from up in his temple. I never knew why Seti would give me those strange looks it, didn't matter to me why he looked at me the way he did, I just thought he was complete jerk. The guard that I was dancing on was my lover from Mitanni. He must have come down to Egypt to be close to me. This man was so damn fine, that it could blow your mine. He had toned muscles nicely solid six packed muscles and he had beautiful golden brown light skin, which glittered in the sun light he captured my heart, and I captured his heart. I could tell when I walked passed his home one day he was standing in the doorway with much love in his eye; he had cute puppy dog eyes when I saw him he made me smile.

"I love you" I said softly to him and smiled back at him and continued on my way home.

As it turns out her wasn't the only man in love with me, the King was also beginning to be attracted to me as well. At, the palace, my lover and some of our friends were just standing around having a good time. I was playing around doing my dancing routine, belly dancing and I was good at it too. I danced upon my love showing him my love and affection. I pranced my butt all up on his penis making him blush with excitement. The crowd was roar in excitement as I danced upon my love meanwhile Seti stood above watching us and drooling over me.

I'm assuming that Tuya was unpleased with how Seti stared at me, as I danced with the guards, because that following night there was a dance ceremony that included Tuya and her lady friend. The ladies danced before Seti, whom enjoyed every bit of the dance. The dance routine that the ladies were performing was identical to the African dances, which I've seen in my present life. Tuya and the other dancers looked their best in their gold and red attire. The gold on their costumes glowed during the night performance, this was truly and astonishing scene, even I had slightly enjoyed it. I guess this was Tuya's way to show her husband that she could do the same for him too.

The job as a household servant wasn't as bad as I thought it would be. Like I've said earlier, sometimes we hardly would do anything but stand around the throne room alongside Seti in case we were needed to carry out an order. Some of us would be placed behind and on the side of Seti where we would laugh and tease him behind his back. One time I got caught laughing at Seti and glared at me, sternly for a very long minute. Seti's glare made me shake in my sandals when he turned around to me, but little did I knew, that Seti was goo-goo eyeing me.

Food had become scarce in our home at one time. My sisters and I were starving and had no food to eat. Ankh, Mery, Setepenre and I sat on the floor crouching down holding are stomachs in our arms, while Tenta'aten sat on a table hungry. Knowing that Seti had feelings for me, I ran to his palace and fell before him begging him for him to help feed me and my sisters. Seti was surprised as I snuck up behind him falling on his blue-green cape. To my luck, he did shortly after, there was a knock at my door I answered, but there was no one there but a bucket of hot bread. I took the bread inside we began to eat on the floor. I joked with Ankh saying "now that's how you get things done" she laughs and so did I. startlingly, I noticed Seti smiling outside our window as well. At that moment, my point was proven.

Besides my four sisters and Beke, there were other family members that were also living in Egypt. Some of them would come and visit us every time that they could get a chance to, and some would come when we least expect them to. At the break of dawn, there was commotion coming from outside my sister's home. People were gathered around in the middle of the street looking down at the ground. My sisters and I awoke and opened the door to find one of our relatives lying in the middle of the street.

Immediately, my sisters weep when they saw this unknown young woman lying appearing lifeless on before them. This girl was within the same age group as Setepenre and myself, but just a few years or a year older than Setepenre. She was a healthy weighted woman. She also had long wavy black hair and very light brown skin like Ankh and Mery. This girl was very attractive just like my other sisters, but she always wore this raggedy black cloak. Who this girl was to me, at the time was a mystery, but it wasn't long for me to figure out that she was. This girl was another one of my sisters, Nefernerferure (Nefer-nefer-u-re). *"The most Beautiful One of Re"* is what her name meant, and what beauty she was. It was unknown where my sister was before she came to my sisters' house, but she was not in very good health.

Almost immediately, my sisters welcome Neferneferure into our home, but she was not alone. There was second woman with her, whom I believed to be Neferneferuaten-Tasherit (Nefer-neferaten Ta-sher-it). Neferneferuaten was my fifth older sister; born after Ankh and Tenta'aten, and before Neferneferure, Setepenre, and myself. Neferneferuaten Tasherit's name meant, *"The Beautiful of the Aten, the younger"* similar to Neferneferure's name meaning, which might also be an indication that the two actually were twins. Neferneferuaten Tasherit was also name after her famous mother, Queen Nefertiti's throne name. Neferneferuaten Tasherit had long curly hair and wore a black dingy rob just like the other woman. These women looked identical to each other and could easily been passed as twins. She looked a little bit older than the other woman. Neferneferure and Neferneferuaten both were the same weight and were also very attractive like her. This was a reunion of siblings.

My sisters and I sat chatting and laughing with each other talking about the old days and catching up where we all last left off. Neferneferuaten, the younger was lying in Neferneferure's lap just giggling. It was obviously so good to see our two sisters again. It was a real pleasure to see our two sisters again. However, there was something really wrong with Neferneferure.

In the middle of the night, Neferneferure woke everyone up, moaning and growing in pain. Mery and Ankh quickly tend to her trying to comfort her and calm her down. Neferneferure's groaning irked my nerves, because I would be trying to get myself some sleep and she would wake up in the middle of the night screaming. "What's wrong?" I asked Ankh "nothing I can't talk to you about" Ankh waved her hand signaling me to lie down and to go back to sleep. Whatever happened to Nefeneferure caused her to be in great deal of pain and me for the least, for preventing me and the rest of us from getting some sleep at night. After this, I didn't get any memories of my two sisters which made me assume that they disappeared.

Now, seeming that many of my memories occurred in Seti's palace, I can say that they were actually were there. Someone had to stay home and watch over Neferneferure, and I believe that's what Neferneferuaten Tasherit did, while the rest of us went off to work. Luckily for them, they didn't have to deal with the rude royals like the rest of us.

Another one of our relatives came to visit us one day. This time, it was our cousin Psetenupe (Sete-Noo-Pay). Psetenupe would come and visit us very frequently, and each time she came she wasn't unpleasant to me. She wasn't so keen with me like she was with my sisters for some unknown reasons and for that reason, is also why I disliked her too. To me, she was very stuck up and uppity. She would give me disgusted looks and sometimes pretended that I wasn't in her presence. A real bitchy woman in my opinion if you asked me

One day, she had the nerve to ask my sisters in front of me "what is he doing here?" my sisters had to explain to her why I was here in Egypt which hopefully she understood. Still, I didn't know why Psetenupe disliked me, but I was beginning to speculate that it had to something to do with my mother and what happened to Lady Nefertiti. Anyhow, Psetenupe did a Houdini and we never saw her for a while. It was good ridings on my part. I was not even concerned that she went away.

There has been vandalism going on lately around the palace on the temples of Seti's father, Ramses I and were getting away with it and that someone was me and my guard lover. One night, we were at it again. We took large branches and scratched a line across the walls of one of Seti's temples. We did this very quickly so no one could catch us I was enjoying every bit of doing this, I was having fun. But I didn't expect what happened to happen next.

As soon as I got to the other corner of this temple, Seti pops out from behind the wall. Seti startled me to death, my friend scurried off home, leaving myself to Seti's wrath, or so I thought. Seti immediately took the stick from my hand and slapped my wrist. "I knew it was you Amenhotep" Seti said with a nice smile "I knew you were the he one vandalizing my father's temples" he grins. How Seti knew was beyond me, but he knew.

As Seti walked closer and closer to me, I tried to back away from Seti, attempting to escape, but there was no way I would have seeming that Seti's broad shoulders was blocking my way to escape. I was going to be in some hot water now. A lot of thoughts went through my head, whether I was going to die, or severely punish for my crime the thoughts were frightening. Seti walked me back to his temple where I met up with one of my sisters, Ankh who was coming home from the palace that night.

Ankh looked lavished that night. Ankh had her hair braided with gold rings attached to her braids, colorful rings on her arm, a beautiful beaded necklace, and a pink cloak covering a percentage of her nice white gowns. Ankh really looked her best that night. Seti told Ankh about me vandalizing his father's temples. Ashamed of my actions, Ankh shook her head. To my surprise, Seti let me go, but my actions wasn't about to go un-dealt with.

For my ill behavior, Ankh told my mother of my actions by writing a letter to her to Mitanni. It was not long for me to get a response back from my mother because the next thing I knew, I got a letter from my mother telling how I should behave myself. The letter stated.

"I was a young prince and should start acting like one". The angered words from my mother got to me like it should, but I was upset with my sister Ankh for snitching on me.

The next evening, Ankh and I got into an argument, about something simple and stupid, possibly because she ratted me out to my mother. The argument got so out of hand, that Seti had to step in and hush the both of us. I rolled my eyes and sucked my teeth still having that bad taste in my mouth for the king-to-be. Eventually, we got over this and we went back to our normal relationship.

In the beginning, I was quite a handful for my sisters, Ankh and Mery pacifically. I was truly acting like the youngest child free-spirited and getting into trouble. One time Ankh and Mery came home to find me dancing on the dinner table, you know doing my belly dancing. My sisters just stood there amazed and surprised at what I was doing. They just stood there watching me. (Laughter) they probably thought I was a weird child.

On an early morning, I was assigned to serve Tuya and her company today. Tuya and her lady friend were eating breakfast. It was very early in the evening when we were standing outside while they ate. What Tuya would do next would hurt my feelings. Tuya knew about my relationship with one of the guards, so she wanted to ponder around with me with the situation. Tuya called upon my Guard lover to her, and she did the unthinkable. Queen Tuya pulls out my lover's penis and placed it in her mouth. Then she looks at me and laughed about and so did her friend. This offended me a lot and all I could do is just stand there and watch. Tuya had one she got me upset highly upset. This made me furious with my love, thinking that he just humiliated me in front of everyone.

My love tried, numerously, to get me to understand that he never intended for Tuya to do what she did, but I didn't want to hear it. For a while, I remained angry with him and I didn't spoke to him for a while. My love constantly tried to beg me for forgiveness but I kept on refusing him, but eventually I forgave him for it. This was one of those events that I tried to avoid because it was too embarrassing, but I felt I had to wright just to get out of mind. For Tuya to do such a thing on her part was disgusting.

It didn't take long for me to be sprawled in my lover's arms again. That night felt his pride penetrate me. It was very painful as he went in and out in me, however, I could understand his deep passion for me. I gripped his muscular back as he moved slowly up and down on me this man knew how to make love. We both enjoyed each other in that moment. That night we felt as if we were being watched by someone from the outside of our hut. We couldn't tell it was very dark outside and cold. Only the cool breeze snuck into the hut like a thief in the night, it may have been Seti that was creeping through the night. After me and my lover made love, we laughed about it and he kissed me. We were in love again, but this sweet reunion was going to be short lived.

My guard lover was there to witness many of Seti's wicked deeds against my family and probably when I wasn't around. On a bright afternoon, Seti's guards were moving the sarcophagus of particular kings and queens that came before Seti and his father. They guards were moving their belongings and treasures to another location. One of those sarcophagi was that of my fathers. Ankh and Mery weep as they carry away my father's coffin they wept "Papa!" on the ground. As the coffin came across me, I placed my hand on top of its golden surface in memory of him. My love asked me "do you miss him?" I replied gently "yes" and looked onward as the guards carried him way. I wondered why were they moving the body of my father and where were they taking him.

Our background as being children of the "Heretic pharaoh" has gotten us into some pretty nasty and unhappy situations. Like Ankh for instance, one late evening she was getting herself all dressed up for her new beau that she was recently seeing. She got all dressed up in gold and wore one of her old white gowns and her royal vulture crown. Ankh had to look her best to hook this new guy and she was very excited about this guy but unfortunately it did not work out due to our family history. That night Ankh was on the ground again crawling backwards from a man, I take it the man she was supposedly had the date with. The man was about to beat her with his hand but then Mery intervened shouting "No!" hitting the man repeatedly and pulling on him. I don't know what Ankh did to upset this guy, but he sure had it out for her. Mery put a decent fight against, the man but she wasn't strong enough to stop him as the man through her to the side. The man yelled at Ankh and then walked away.

I felt really bad for Ankh that this happened to her especially when she had that sad look on her face. That night Ankh cried in the lap of Mery whom groomed her nice curly long hair trying to calm her down, both of my sisters wore their hair out. I stood afar watching them, from the living room feeling sympathetic to Ankh and what happened to her. Perhaps someday, I thought, she would get someone to marry her.

This wasn't my first encounter with this aggressive man. On a late afternoon, possibly after I've finished my work in the palace, I came back home to find Ankh lying in bed (fully clothed) and making out with this same guy. For a moment, the two didn't notice that I was standing there until Ankh's beau looked up. Noticing the look on her lover's face, Ankh turns around and screams when she saw me standing there. What a shock that must have gave her.

Ankh had her turn to frighten me back. On a cloudy gray day Ankh and I was sitting outside our house chatting with each other. Ankh told me to look down I didn't know what to expect but Ankh lifts her dress shouting

"Raaah!" Ankh screams revealing her ugly feet.

Ankh's feet were in the most horrible condition that I've ever seen that it frightened me. Ankh laughs at me afterwards. Looking at Ankh's feet was disgusting and it made me mad that she showed me her feet.

On another occasion Ankh and Mery watched as Seti's men removed the names of several kings and Queens of times past off a black stone wall. These Kings were my father's and his successors, which included Tutankhamen and Smenkhare. Mery and Ankh whimpered as they slowly removed each name. Later on that evening in our home, my sisters were hurt by this, Mery sat in a chair in upon a table facing a wall with her head in her hand sobbing. Ankh stood behind her trying to comfort her and then she turned to me and asked "Why would they do this to us?" Ankh asked but I didn't had answer for this

On a bright afternoon, Mery and I took a trip to north of our home to a place that we once called home, Akhetaten, the now ruined city that our father built during both of our childhood. When we arrived to Akhenaten, there was almost nothing left of our old home, Mery got out of the chariot to gaze out at of the area where she grew up at and where I was born. Mery's eyes filled with many memories and saddened lost she stood there for a moment in silence, lost in memory of her former childhood home.

Mery always talked to me about her past and how good it was. One of the things that she always talked about was her beloved former husband Smenk as she called him. I remember one evening, Mery and I was sitting chatting about the same subject. Mery told me how our father arranged her marriage between this Smenk and how good he was to her until an incident happened that tore them apart, she blamed the priests for what happened to her Smenk. Mery was always proud to share her stories with me and I was eager to listen to them. I could tell from her eyes that she was saddened by their outcome.

My sister's would always talk about their childhood and how good it was and their stories never bored me. One person that my sisters loved to talk about was our sister Mek. Mek originally, was my second oldest sister, being younger than Mery and older than; Ankh, Tentenaten, Setepenre, and of course myself. I never got to know my big sister, as she died before we got to know each other. Exactly, right before I was born. Mery and Ankh told me what happened to Mek. According to Ankh and Mery, Mek ate bad grapes, and suddenly fell sick. That day they discovered that she was sick she fell to the ground her mother and everyone was surprised.

"Mek!" Nefertiti called out to her in horror, but Mek did not move. Then shortly after this, Mek died.

Ankh and Mery said that our father had every grape tree that was growing in our city thrown out and burned. Mery said that they were all piled up by the mass. The thought of this dark memory saddened my two sisters. "I miss her" Mery says "I miss her too" Ankh replies softly. Ironically, I was eating grapes that same night when I received this vision. Man I took a good look at the grape that I was preparing in my mouth and said "Grapes can kill you to?" and continued to eat.

Months later, in this life, I got a bug (but not from the grapes). Being ill made me thought of Mek and how she must have felt in her last days. She must have been in great pain just like I was probably throwing up everywhere and barely could eat a thing. Sadly, unlike me, Mek did not recovery from her illness and lost her life. Because of this, I've learned to be even more careful of what I eat. When these memories first started to rain upon me, I believed that Meketaten (Mek-et-aten), the second daughter of Akhenaten and Queen Nefertiti was my mother, even though the visions showed me otherwise that Queen Kiya was the woman that I called mother in my past life. I was really stuck on Nefertiti and the royal family then, and it took me a while to except what I've been shown. Mek was the person that my father and Nefertiti were grieving that day at the ceremony. Perhaps, I reminded or held a strong resemblance to Mek.

My mother must have heard from my sisters about all the terrible things that Seti was doing to us from my sisters, because news broke across the town of a plot involving my mother. One grey day I opened the door to find a message written in stone. The message read "Kiya seeks El a gala." Whom or whatever the El a gala was a mystery to me. But whatever my mother was trying to do must have failed, because the next thing that she would do, no one would see coming.

A surprising event caught us off guard. One day, while we were home. My mother came to visit us. Mery and Ankh were very enlightened by her sudden appearance and ran to hug her. My mother wore her beautiful Nubian wig, a white gown that was white as snow and she wore a golden crest around her gown, my mother looked magnificent. Mery and Ankh greeted my mother with hugs. The first question that came out of my mother's mouth was, "where's Tentenaten?" as she pronounced my full sister's name. Ankh replied softly "she was not here." Tenta'aten wasn't present when our mother arrived in Egypt she was nowhere to be found.

The last time, Mother, Tenta'aten, and myself were together was at one of my father's celebrations at Akhetaten, our father's former city. Tenta'aten and I was part of a parade. While I was marching on, Tenta'aten was walking beside my mother wearing a little white gown, a solid gold head band, and Nubian style wig. Mother was sitting in a canopy that was being carried by her strong guards. After this, well, you already know the rest.

To our surprises, my mother had come to meet with Seti in order for him to allow us to leave with her from Egypt. This got us all excited especially my sisters. Finally our troubles were going to end, or so we all thought. Soon after, we met with Seti, who was sitting on his throne with his mother standing next to him. My mother stood very close to me while my sisters stood behind us waiting for the outcome of this meeting. My mother's presence was so strong that I could feel it as I envisioned it and her gown lit up as the ray from the sun shined upon it. My mother looked very amazing that evening.

My eldest sisters stood behind us, patiently awaiting Seti's choice to set us free so they can be finally relieved them of their painful memories. Seti angrily refused to let us go, which shook my sisters into tears. Seti was so angry that my mother would ask him such a thing, possibly because she threatened to take me from him. The king ordered my mother to never return back to Egypt. This left my mother standing in complete shock and upset about the whole thing. Mother was ordered to leave the temple immediately. As mother walks away she turns to take one final look upon me and I saw the hurt upon her face and in her eyes. Finally, she walks away leaving my sisters sobbing and I battered with grief. We were too never seeing her again. Although, this hurt my sisters, it hurt me the most. My mother was gone from my life and this evening turn from exhilarating to devastating.

As soon as my mother left, I ran after her crying out "Momma!" trying to leave with her but by the time I made it out of the temple, mother was gone. Immediately, when we came home, I quickly snatched up the little stuff I had in order to try and catch up with my mother. I had to hurry up and catch her, because I didn't want her to leave me alone. "Amenhotep no" Neferneferure says softly, weeping as well. Neferneferure held her face in her hands distraught just as much as I was. I tried to look for her carriage but she was gone. Unable to find my mother, I came home crying my eyes out. I slid down our house wall crying heavily, and I stayed there for a long moment. I could only imagine how my mother must have felt being banished away from her only two children she probably cried out as much as I did, but even more.

It was my fault why this was happening, why we couldn't leave Egypt. If Seti was never in love with me, we probably would have been permitted to go. Perhaps, the reason why the Pharaoh didn't permit my sisters to leave is because of him knowing how much my sisters meant to me. Thus, he didn't want me to feel alone and left out so she ordered them stay or it could have been that they were valuable servants and he didn't want to lose them.

After my outburst of tears, some village people came knocking on our door to see how I was doing. Ankh answers with a smile" oh he's alright his great uncle calmed him down" she implies but I was far from okay. I lied in the bed utterly shocked about losing my mother must have been laying there thinking what I'm going to do without my mother now that she was banished away from my life.

This memory still makes me weep to this very day. Imagine having your mother being banished away from you, one would cry too. But, I didn't lose my mother because I returned to her in this life. In this life my mother and I are not the best of friends. When we are younger we believe that our parents are pure gold and nothing that they ever do is wrong. Well for me, that wasn't the case. Unlike my younger siblings, I was the one who was most distant from both my parents. I basically grew in fear of my mother and everyone around me. Anyone who had caused even the slightest pain in my life, I tried to stay away from, but then again, I had to deal with because I had to have a place to live. There has been some sweet days between the two of us, and I'm hoping we could have some more. But, I forgive my mother for the wrong that she has done "no cold heart here."

My mother taught me the greatest lessons in life, really didn't know it. My mother and no one ever knew this, but at thirteen years old I wanted to commit suicide. I was being bullied harshly in school, I felt as if the only way I could end my suffering is to just die. The thought of killing myself in my back yard rooted deeply in my head. But, I remembered these words my mother muttered a while back "you are a punk if you decide to kill yourself." What my mother meant, was that you are only allowing those people whom you feel are superior to you succeed, and I wasn't going to allow that to happen

No one is going to claim victory over me, and I didn't do it. Even later on down the line, when those suicide thoughts would come up, I would remember what my mother told me. I would like to say this to those people whom done me so wrong." You can keep that old Terrell, you can beat him up, and even toss him around, but you can't have this new Terrell, oh no ma'am, no sir. Hence, if you dare try, or even attempt to take him from me, you're going to have to fight, because I'm not giving this new Terrell up." I'm the victor of this battle.

Because of these beautiful memories; I've learned to forgive people, even though I may not be doing the wrong all the time. It's because of this story that I no longer hate my mother, I'm lucky to have her again at all. Despite, how things were between us, I wouldn't have anyone else be my mother, NO ONE! This is not the second time me and my mother have crossed paths in another lifetime, but that's another story.

Due to our poor living conditions, my sisters and I had to make sacrifices that we didn't want to make just so the all of us could have food to eat. One time, Ankh wanted a pair of golden small jiggling earrings she saw, while we were at the market place. However, Mery took the earrings away and told Ankh "no". We were scarce on money as it was, and Mery didn't want any of the money to be wasted on foolish items such as ear rings. Angry, Ankh pouts wrapping her arms around each other and looking down to the ground. "We have to be careful with our spending" Mery stressed as she and Ankh rumble through the goods on the market table. Ankh was still very unsatisfied by the lifestyle she was living and she made it very clear later on.

"I hate it!" Ankh yells out at Mery and my Tenta'aten, hating this peasant life we were all living. Setepenre and Tenta'aten felt sympathetic in how Ankh was feeling and couldn't say much of anything to comfort Ankh themselves. Perhaps, they too were feeling the same way deep within themselves, I know for a fact that I did.

When it came to us needing money again, it was Tentenaten this time that felt the sting of sacrifice. Ankh and Tenta'aten were arguing over a little pale blue green marble artifact that was in my Tentenaten's hands.

"Give it to me!" Ankh repeats herself to Tentenaten "stop!" Tentenaten yells repeatedly at Ankh then she outbursts "Stop Ankh!" thus Ankh stops and Tentenaten prevailed in keeping this object.

Apparently, this object belonged to Tenta'aten and she didn't want to give it up. Whatever it was she was holding in her hands, she seemed very distraught about it. This mysterious object had to be something worth bickering over. I take it that this precious thing was a gift to my third sister to just like father's Golden arm band and just like it she cherished it so.

Soon that day came when someone else would be taken away from me. One day, I was looking for my love, but he was nowhere to be found no one knew what really happen to my lover. There were rumors that he left and that Seti may have had him killed for some unknown reason, possibly to get to me. After this I was shown what had happened to my lover he was buried just outside the city gates, perhaps by those whom were sent by Seti to have him killed.

Deep inside, I knew for a fact, Seti had my lover killed off just so he could get closer to me. I was very heartbroken about the loss of my lover one moment he was there and the next moment he was gone. The very thought of his death upset me I didn't want to believe what everyone was telling about what had really happened to him but deep down inside I did, this caused me to hate the Seti even more.

Miraculously, I got the opportunity to meet my guard lover again in this life. Oh my god is he ever so fine just as he was in my present life. I didn't catch it at first until I had to replay those memories back in my mind. It is unfortunate that his heart belong to someone else and not made for me in this lifetime. Knowing what I know about him made me slip back in love with him and it hurts to know that there will never be an us, yet another person from that lifetime that may never know how much he means to me. It's all good though, at least someone else could have those wonderful experiences that I had with this man's beautiful soul. This significant lover is able to laugh and cry just as I did my best wished to them.

As for me, I'm waiting for that special person to make that special appearance in my life. As a matter of fact, I was on a quest to find love and so far what I've found wasn't love. I haven't given up on love just yet there is someone out there waiting for me I just know it and I'm out there just searching for him. I think I'm going to wait patiently for this guy this time around but my love will never change for my guard lover though he will still have a special little place in my heart.

Now that my lover was out of the picture, this gave Seti the opportunity he needed to get next to me. I would go pray at the gods every morning. Before I enter the temple, I would have a bowl with a candle in it to take to the statue with its hand out as if it was begging I would take off my shoes and pray. Anyone who wanted to enter the temple had to remove their shoes. Seti would be there watching me, from the shadows pleased at my devotion of the gods we spoke a few words and I didn't stay long because I didn't want to be in the same room with the man who had my beloved lover killed. I hated Seti greatly for it, and he knew it. Despite my rude behaviors, and my rude actions towards Seti, it did not stop him from trying to make his move on me. Seti was just as they say, warming up.

To make their Dynasties flourish, all Pharaohs are expected to have a male heir. Seti and Tuya were trying to accomplish this but unfortunately, they were not successful as they lost their first son. I was there at the funeral service, Seti and Tuya was very emotional about the loss of their son, who was about five or six when he died. Seti was leaned over crying over the mummy of their son. The room was crowed and filled smoke filled the air as the priests commit the funeral service. This was an uncomfortable and sad movement. The event it made me think about my love and how I longed to be with him at the moment. Because of my loss, I began to drift off from many of my new friends and stayed to myself. Deeply, I was missing my love so much that it was hard to live life without him or being with someone else. But my mourning stage was about to come an end.

One cool day, I was walking alongside a huge pond or lake. That day I wore a gorgeous white gown and rob with gold designs on them. I also wore my father's golden wristband I looked like royalty that afternoon. My entire attire glistened in the Aten's rays as I looked up to the sky. I looked up and noticed that the king was watching from the up top on a ridge, I paid him no mind like I always do, until I slipped up into the water where I lost my bracelet. I didn't know that there was a crocodile swimming inside it as I reached for my bracelet, the creature sprang up out of the water at me. Seti came to stop me from getting me hand bitten off by the crocodile. In a fit, I tried pushed Seti away from me, but he managed to calm me down after wards, softly I thanked him (with my head turned from him) and walked off. That was the last time I saw my father's bracelet, it was lost in the depth of those waters for good. However, I guarantee that it's still there.

Even now, I still have a bad habit of losing something, I wouldn't be surprise if Egyptologists finds anything that belonged to me, because I'm good for losing anything.(Chuckling) I wouldn't be surprise if someone find something around town that is mines because I don't keep up with nothing, seriously.

That night, Mery and Ankh were dancing in front of a warm fire with some men that I believed were guards. Mery and Ankh loved to celebrate; I think the two of them were known for celebrating. While my two sisters were dancing the night away around a fire and men, I was cleaning dishes and picking at leftovers off their plates that's when Seti appeared in a black rob in our home. Seti came to speak with me about that moment at the lake, and to see if I was okay. Gently, I exchanged an answer to him we talked for a brief moment. I tried not to pay attention him, because I was still mad at him for having my love killed that year ago. Seti then approached me from behind and started to rub me on my back and pressed up on me. Softly, I felt his penis rise up on the walls of my butt. From the way it felt, it was a decent size. It pleased me the way Seti was touching me, rubbing me in all the right places. Seti was breathing down my neck. Seti rubbed his face against mines and his breath was very warm and comforting. If we had the chance, we probably would have made love in that kitchen.

During the heat of the moment, Ankh came and saw Seti all up on me which made Seti stopped in an instant. I didn't know what just happened, but it made me started to like Seti. "The king actually does care about me" I must have thought. It was not long for me to stop grieving over my former lover, because Seti made my pain go away. He made happy again, he made me feel loved. Ankh knew this and didn't like that idea.

One early morning, several servants including Setepenre and myself, came into the throne room to see Seti slapping Ankh down on the floor. Ankh tried to back away from Seti, begging him for mercy, as if she had did something wrong. Although we didn't know what really happened to led to this moment, I knew it had something to do with me. I saw Seti holding pieces of papyrus, a piece of paper the ancients used to write on, in his hand and it sounded like Ankh was trying to do something with them but I don't know what. Whatever was written on those sheets of papyrus must have been very important for Ankh to try to take them from the Pharaoh.

"Are you trying to destroy my kingdom?" Seti yells at Ankh. "No!" Ankh repeats in fear of what Seti might do to her. This event left us other servants baffled as to what Ankh was trying to do. Later during the nighttime, I've asked my love about these papers that he took from Ankh earlier. Seti claimed that he did what he had to do to protect the kingdom. Tears slowly flow from Seti eyes as I spoke with him. Again, I didn't understand what was going on at the time, but I assured Seti that it was alright and never spoke of this incident again.

While I was sleeping one night, in my apartment, I had this awkward dream. I was gliding on through an ancient Egypt tomb. There were statutes of jackals all lined up side by side. Each of them was growling at me as I passed them by. Then standing in the mist of the room was a beautiful Egyptian woman. She wore a white gown and had jewels streaming down here that were connected to a crown. The woman told me that "he lied to you". I asked her "what did Seti lied to me about?" And she kept saying "he lied to you" and then suddenly I woke up. I understand clearly that the woman was talking about Seti and that he had lied to me about my family.

My hint from this dream was that even though the Rammesides (Referring to those of the Ninetieth dynasty and descendants of Ramses I) now had the throne, I was still very much in line to be Pharaoh. Thus, my sister Ankh was trying to prove that to me. This vision made me believe further that I might have belonged to Egyptian royalty, and all possibilities kept pointing directly to the Amarna Family.

Eager to see my new found lover, I attempted to rush out of my sister's home (one late afternoon). Before I could get to the door, Beke asked "Are off to see Seti? " It utterly surprised me that Beke knew about me and Seti, but I already had a clue who might have told her. Ankh and Mery stood in the far corner waiting for an answer to seep from my lips. "No" I responded softly, lying to them and scurrying off. I didn't want to tell my sisters and Beke the truth because I knew if I did, they would stop me from seeing Seti and I wasn't going to allow that to happen.

Ankh and Mery knew full in well what was going on in the bedroom of Seti. One very late and dark night Ankh and Mery got me up from a comfortable sleep to go to the palace. "Seti wishes to see you?" Mery says. So off the three of us went to Seti's palace. There in the dark Seti sat with his eyes closed on his throne just waiting for me. My sisters left me where I stood but I noticed the look on Mery's face as it she knew what was about to happen next. There was no doubt in my mind that neither of my sisters liked this, but there was nothing I they could do. I was Seti's and he was mine.

One evening unexpectedly, there were loud screams coming from the room where Sitre was. Everyone rushes to the room to find Beke attacking Sitre for unknown reasons. One of the guards tried to pull back Beke, who was hitting on the Sitre and pulling on her hair. Beke's action cost herself her life thus she was to be executed immediately after this event.

Beke stood on top of a stone in front of a screaming crowd of civilians. Beke took off her cloak exposing her diseased riddled body to everyone. Ankh and Mery tried helplessly, while trying to bombard their way through the crowd to get Beke down from the stone, but there was nothing that they could have done Beke was going to die. Beke's last words were, "One day they would see the return of the Aten." This infuriated the Ramses, thus with a strong wave of the arm, Beke hung to death.

My sisters looked away as her body swung back and forth. A guard emerges from the crowd with a torch lighting Beke's body up into flames; I assume that no one wanted to touch her diseased body so it was a proper thing to do to have her burned. But, I've learned that any crime against the king or any of his relatives is a crime against the Gods, thus sometimes a proper burial wasn't rewarded to the criminal. Horrified, Ankh screamed in horror as Beke's body burned. That night my sisters and I sat around silently to ourselves thinking of what we could have done to save Beke's life but no matter how we would go back and forth in our minds about the matter, we would have had a run in with the Royal family and neither of us wanted to go head to toe with them. The Rammesides were our rivals, but they has the upper hand on us since they had more force and power. My sisters and I were even lucky to still be breathing.

It really hurt my sisters that Beke was gone and it even hurt me. I think Beke was fed up with the Rammesides, the court, and wished that it returned to the days of my father, when she could worship the Aten but unfortunately it did not happen while she was alive and neither in that time frame but the day did come. Furthermore, this was not the last time that I would run into Beke, oh no we would cross paths again but that too is another story. Sometimes in life you find yourself "Bouncing back" to square one and finding yourself needing those whom you've hurt and thought less off let me put it like that. I'm so thankful from bringing me back from the Darkness.

I think Beke, herself, privately practiced Atenism as so my sisters, especially Mery. Like Akhenaten, Beke might have been a devoted believer of the Aten. So in a way, Beke should be considered the world's first saint and should be remembered for it. Beke's life was a tragic life from the start but in the end she was finally relieved of her pain and was finally able to meet her god.

Today, I have seen Beke clean from her disease. What a powerful and beautiful in essence, as formable as her former mother Queen Tiye. Her smile could light up a whole room and her laugh would make you laugh. She's doing so swell again without her and her husband opening a door for me I wouldn't know where I would be. Heck, I was the sick one this time around and being within her program has helped me a lot and it's with great gratitude that I thank her. Every time I see this woman, I have long glares and smiling thinking about how I use to know her and how beautiful she has become. Most of time I find myself boasting about how great she is and I even told someone that "I love her like me aunt and she is very dear to me" and the reasons is because she once was. Even though we die and move on to another life time or eternal happiness. Did you know that our family from our past life is still our family? I'm sure one has heard you're stuck with the same relatives for eternity. Well that saying is very true.

Beke is very dear to me. I'm so glad that something good came after her life in Egypt because she truly deserved serenity after all she had been through. I'm so glad that I got another chance to make up for the lost time that we never have and to see her smiling face again.

To Beke, keep doing what you doing and someday you will forever be remember for it kindness like yours don't ever be forgotten. I don't know if I would even have the stomach to do what you and your husband does every day but it's like you said "a strong will can take you further down the line" (Beke-reincarnate) and maybe I can say someone's life.

"A New Era Has Been Born"

I believe that there was a bit of confrontation between Seti and some foreign country, because something happened to him that was totally unexpected to everyone. It was very late at night at the palace, almost everyone was asleep, but we soon were awaked by screaming coming from Seti's sleeping chamber. Tuya was screaming her lungs out as Seti was being taken away by two strange men dressed in what looked to me like roman gladiator armor; the two guys went off with Seti in the night. The next morning we arrived to the area where Seti was taken to find him bound, in chain, by hands and foot in the middle of what appeared to me as a coliseum. Seti was wearing a dingy torn greyish cloak and in tears. I ran down to the first row shouting out to Seti. Seti raised his hand towards me and shouting out my name, but there was little I could do.

I think Seti's father might have been able to bail him out and give his captives what they wanted because Seti was freed and was able to return home. I remember that night when he returned home it was dark out and I was standing in the hallway concerned for the prince. Seti and some guards walked passed me from another passage way. Seti didn't say anything to me or even looked at him. I probably thought that he was made at me because I didn't help him. I felt really bad that I couldn't helped him back at the coliseum

I dismissed this lot in my mind and didn't even want to add this part to my book simply because I thought I this could never have happen Seti's the king of Egypt nothing could happen to the Pharaoh especially with all his powerful guards walking around his palace.

Compared to my present life as an Egyptian servant, the world was just as bad as it now. The same old stuff keeps reoccurring over and over again and the thing about it is that these events never get old. There were the usual rich, who thought they were better than the poor, and of course, the wars between the nations. There was all of that, but compared to today, many things of the past have and still remain in secret. No one was all in your business you could kill someone without even being caught, not saying that's a good thing and all but yeah you all get the picture.

The time had come when the old pharaoh, Ramses I, had passed away. At dawn, I watched Seti lean down over and kissing his father one final time. Before Ramses's body was taken for burial, Ramses laid on a stone table just outside the temple alone for some unknown reasons. It was just Seti and I at this place. I stood afar watching Seti mourn his dead father and the beautiful sun set behind them.

Life continued on around the palace shortly after Ramses death. Seti was soon to become the new king of Egypt. The ceremony for the Seti's crowing was beautiful and magnificent. The Pharaoh was dressed in the finest gold and clothing in the country. Seti glistened like a star that evening. Queen Tuya too looked amazing with her gold attire and bright gown. Seti took Tuya's hand and declare them King and Queen of Egypt. Instantly after this, everyone cheered and show their respects to their new King and Queen. However, despite Seti's rise to power, he had not quite over losing his father.

On another late afternoon, at sun set, Seti and I were surrounded by burgundy draperies seated in a tented area in the temple. We sat on the finest burgundy pillows playing chest. Seti had on a beautiful Egyptian bracelet and lay back on the opposite corner of me. My Seti looked so damn good with his nicely build chest. Seti looked as if something was bothering him. Concerned, I attempted to find out what was bothering my love so much to make him sob. "What's wrong?" I asked my over Seti simply stated "I am Seti" stating that nothing could phase his greatness. Later on, when I returned back to the room, was Seti lying down on these very pillows crying his eyes out. Right then and there, I knew that Seti was crying over the loss of his father. Queen Sitre came to her son's cry and sat next to him on a chair. "What's the matter with you?" she asks and it became known what was bothering him. Queen Sitre sat and comforts her son, drying his tears from his wet face.

The loss of his father did not allow Seti to falter on taking on his father's legacy. Soon after his grieving stage, Seti was ready to rule. I've seen many rulers and traders come in and out Seti's palace from all over the western world. It was an amazing experience; I've seen many different people and their type of fashions and gold. Seti was quiet known to other rulers around the continent especially the east. Seti and these rulers would talk on many occasions about trade and other royal matters in the country.

Now that my relationship with Seti was starting to grow, the king allowed me to get involved with his royal affairs. There was yet another meeting to be held in the palace but this time Seti, whom I stood very close to, allowed me to speak. Here came this hideous man whom appeared almost sickly his eyes were pale blue almost as if they glow in the light. This man wore a black shredded cloak over his body he was really nasty looking.

Just when I was about to speak, the strange man asked Seti, "Do you always have your servants speak for you?" Seti replied by stating "He is one of the Amarna." Seti implied that I was of 18th dynasty royalty. The ugly man looked surprised and glared me up and down speechless. Apparently, the man knew of my family, but to me he was just a new face, a face that I wanted to forget.

There was this important meeting going on in the evening in Seti's throne room. The King had his soldiers standing side by side lined up in the direction towards Seti's throne with a spear in one and a brown shield in the other. The men also wore these short wigs, which from my point of view look ridiculous. It appeared that these mean were getting prepared for war or battle, but with whom. Whoever it is must have done something to upset the royals. Seti had announced an offer to one of the soldiers to take the lead. A warrior on the right side on the mid-near end stepped forward and took the pharaoh's offer. Shortly afterwards the meeting was done and Seti sent the men marching out of the throne with the warrior leading them at the side. This event may be in response to the mysterious people whom captured Seti. The king must have wanted his revenge for his public humiliation, and he was soon going to get it.

"The Secret Chamber"

"Many of the world's greatest secrets are locked within the back of your mind just waiting to be revealed to the world."

Seti and Tuya, were trying to make another son to replace the son that they have already lost instead they got a beautiful daughter Tia. Queen Tuya would often go up to northern Egypt, perhaps to Cairo to do her queen duties which would leave the king to fulfill his wishes. Little did we all know, that she was pregnant at the time with her second son, Ramses II, Even though Tuya was Seti's Queen, she barely was around like she was before. I mean Tuya would go up to Upper Egypt every time she got the chance for whatever reasons were unknown.

Seti and Tuya have been together for a number of years. Perhaps, since they were teenagers. I wasn't there for their wedding ceremony, but I imagine how their wedding might have been. I guarantee that it was very beautiful. Seti and Tuya probably looked their finest that day with all the finest gold and jewelry on. I bet their ceremony was huge hosted by the High Priest of Amun and their parents. Seti's father probably gave a brief speech giving his best wishes to the newlyweds. Finally, after Ramses's speech, the two say their vows and the priest announced them husband and wife. That must have been the greatest day of their lives. Which brings me back to this question, why me? Of all the beautiful Egyptian woman, Female royalties, nobles, and even female servants that were running around in that time. Why was Seti so interested in me? Perhaps it was not our similarities that attracted him to me.

Seti had gotten his chance to get close to me and every little time that he had he made sure that it was with me. It seems as if he spent more time with me than in his own wife. The first thing we did was made love. For the very first time, we were in each other's arms. Literally, we lay in bed one night wrapped up in white silk blankets. Like my lover before him, Seti was good in bed; he knew all the right tricks and ways to make you scream. First I sat in Seti's laps gripped tight in his muscled arms tongue kissing Seti. Seti then laid my body down on the bed to have sex some more. Sex with Seti was beautiful and pleasing after that breathe taking moment, we talked for a moment I was wrapped around his arms and I placed my fingers on his large wet lips then before we know it we were sleeping in each other's arms. It felt very good to be loved again

After this, Seti and I would have sex a numerous of times. Seti's bedroom was our sexual playground. Seti's bed room was like a suite, it was designed and suitable for the king and Queen. Seti's king-size bed laid smack dab on in the middle of the floor, literally. There was nothing holding it up from the ground, it was like a large and wide mattress on the floor.

Seti was a very passionate love maker, and enjoyed every bit of my body. He enjoyed it so much, that he would go right ahead and placed me on all fours, pulling up my clothing. One night after love making, I heard chariots from the outside, so I went to see who that might be riding into town.

A long string of Seti's sperm stretched from my bosom from the tip of Seti's penis. Seti just laid there biting his lips, enjoying the scenery. I watched in pleasure as the charioteers rode into the city. Seti just kept on lying there just mesmerized at my body, pacifically my butt. "That's mine now" Seti probably thought to himself and in his mind, he was right

Seti and I became deep compassionate lovers. Because of this, I was lifted up the ranks. Seti and I were now equals. Together like king and Queen, we sat side by side, never moving a budge from each other's side. We would discuss important matters such as; designs on Seti's latest projects, which were his temples. When building production was slow, it made me very impatient. A problem came up with the productions of one of the projects and like spoiled Tuya had a fit. I remember yelling at the scribe telling him to "get it done". Then Seti halted me to stop. Only Seti knew how to fix this problem and whatever he said must have worked because the next thing I knew, one of our temples was already half way finished

During the construction of the Temples, Seti took me to one of his new unfinished temples. We were so amazed me how well everything was coming along. Then Seti took me to one of the column and carved are names in it, as a symbol stating that this temple belonged to the both of us. Seti took me several places including to his place of burial in the valley known as the Valley of the Kings.

Seti's tomb was so beautiful inside and extremely large. It was filled with vibrant colors and scenes on its walls depicting, stories about Seti's life and battles before he became the new Pharaoh Seti also shown me another chamber of the tomb that was completely untouched and never used. Seti told me that when we both die, we would then be both buried together, together even in death. This brought a pleased smile upon my face.

Many have said that there were many great secrets buried in the sands of Egypt, and they were right and I was going to get my chance to know a great secret. One day, the Pharaoh took me out to a strange looking door which was connected to a secret chamber. Seti told me that only the kings of Egypt have knowledge of this chamber and the secret of this chamber dies with them. He told me that this chamber also contains some of Egypt's ancient secrets. To get inside, Seti had to perform a secret code which was in the form of three knocks. Set knocked first at the top middle of the door, then southwest of the door then directly to the left, as if he was making a perfect triangle out of his knocks. Once he made his final knock the sealed stone carved door opened. It was like magic when it opened itself up.

Inside this mysterious hidden chamber, there was a pathway that led to two pathways on the left and another of the right. The pathway on the left was a trap, a large boulder with sharp spikes would swung out of nowhere and crush any who had no permission to enter this chamber. This entire chamber was well set up with traps I almost came very close to being crushed by that spiked boulder had it weren't for Seti, saving me I surely would have met my demise. Next we made our way to the right, the correct way down the chamber. There was a staircase that led to an open room. But before we went down the flight of stairs, Seti took me to a very small room where we made love, Seti sat in his masculine arms kissing and rubbing his nicely chiseled back. There in that room, I left a silk cape that had golden lining on it.

After love making, Seti and I continued down the path of stairs into the open room. I saw an unwrapped body of a strange being. This body was not of human being. By the shape of its head and how wide the eye sockets were, they were very huge unlike most human's eye sockets that I've ever seen. The body gave off a fowl stench unlike anything I've ever smelted before the smell lit up the room. Whoever, this person was he was of great importance to the Pharaohs of the past and present. Beyond this non-human figure there were lots of gold sitting behind it.

There was this huge unidentified object sitting before the corpse. These strange large objects belonged to the being that was lying on the stone table before us; he may have come here from the stars. There has been many evidence and theories that suggested that ancient man have been visited by alien life forms from space. These life forms have been mistaken as gods from the skies when really; they are beings from other world. Many have argue about this matter whether or not that this is true or not for we will never know if this is fact, but whatever the case may be, the machine that I saw wasn't a manmade object.

Sitting amongst the unknown object, was the golden tip of the third pyramid, it was said to match the brightest star of the Orion's belt for whatever reasons, this beautiful artifact was kept inside this chamber, possibly to prevent thieves from stealing it, or another crash landing of some sort. After, we left the chamber, I was told never to tell anyone about what I saw in this chamber, and I kept my promise ever since.

My moments with Seti were always so sweet. We would always have a good time when we were together. One time Seti decided to play hide and peek. He kept running back and forth behind me trying to chase me down. That evening Seti wore this ruby and sapphire outfit on that appeared to have sapphire Egyptian papyrus flowers on it. Seti even had the cloak to match his outfit; Seti looked very decent that evening. The outfit that I wore was just as spectacular as Seti's. It was a fine white gown with gold attributes on it. Seti had me dressed with the finest gold and sapphire jewelry in the country.

Seti always made sure that I was dressed in the finest material and jewelry in the country. On a special occasion, Seti had me dressed up for a festivity, which he was having in his throne room. I was dressed in the finest clothing and jewels that I've probably ever worn in that life. As I opened the entrance to the throne room, all eyed gazed upon me. Everyone that was staring at me was completely astonished as to how I looked. I could still feel the nervous feeling in my stomach, that I felt when I walked into the room. As I walked further into the room, I could see Seti standing at his throne smiling. Seti's big smile made me smile and happy. Suddenly, my nervous feelings went away

THE CRUSHING MOMENT

As time progressed, our relationship had become profound, even more serious in our relationship than we ever were. My love for Seti intensified tenfold, and I could resist him. Thoughtlessly, I thought our love would stand strong forever and nothing could break our bond, but much to my bitter sweet dismay, it wouldn't. The moment of truth was about to arrive, and a moment that I failed see coming.

I failed to realize that Seti wasn't only my love. Seti was still with Tuya. The both of us were sharing him, but only one of us would have him in the end, and in the end it was Tuya. She was pregnant at the time of my Seti's love quarrel, and I was unaware of it.

One early morning, I awoke with a smile on my face, totally excited about this new day, which Seti and I were going to share. Suddenly, I heard loud cheering coming from the outside. Everyone was gathered up in the center of the town for some unknown reason. It appeared as though as everyone was expecting the arrival of someone, that someone was Tuya, but she was not alone. In a horse drawn chariot, Seti and Queen Tuya rode into town with their new bundle of joy. In her arms held Ramses II, Seti's successor and the child that would become one of Egypt's most powerful rulers. Many of you might be familiar with Ramses II from the biblical story of the Exodus as the pharaoh that refused to allow Moses people to be free; well this little guy was him.

Seti sat in his chariot, proud and delighted of his new born son. Seti was so overjoyed that he showed everyone in the entire city his new baby boy by lifting him up into the air for everyone in the city to see. Everyone, but me, was overwhelmed and happy about the arrival of this new prince.

At this very moment, it was the end of the line for me. Attempting to stir Seti's attention towards me, I called out Seti's several times to get his attention finally he responded by yelling something to me that, in that moment, shattered my soul and all connections to the king.

"Back away from me servant!" Seti points to me.

My feelings were hurt when Seti muttered out those words. Me, the son of Tadukhipa and Akhenaten a servant, how dare him. More so, how dare he turned on me like he did. This was a truly embarrassing and very painful moment.

Immediately, my heart dropped. Those very words broke me into tears. Everyone in the area started yelling and shouting at me, to back away from their Pharaoh. My sisters watched as my whole world was crashing down. From the looks over their eyes, they could have felt my pain. My sisters knew full and well what was happening, I might go even further and say that they knew that I was going to meet my downfall someday.

After that embarrassing moment, the King announced that he and his queen were going to have a celebration in honor of their new born son back at their home shortly afterwards Seti road off in his chariot with his son at hand and Tuya. While everyone followed the royal couple back to their palace, I slowly walked back to my home in self-pity crying my broken heart out.

Later on, my sisters attempted to cheer me up. "It's going to be alright" Ankh pats my back as we walked back to our home. But she was wrong, everything wasn't alright. The world that Seti and I built upon, us was no more now that Ramses was here. Once again I found myself alone and heartbroken but this time I've lost someone internally.

Time went on, and once again, I've had become a mere servant. Things went back to the way things were before Seti and I fell in love.

He had one my hatred yet again and I had won back his non interest. Not only was I unhappy, but I was also angry, outraged at Seti for making a fool out of me and for taking my heart and shoving it into the dirt and stomping on it. I never felt so betrayed in my life. Seti's main focus was his son and we barely spoke, not even when he would give me commands. I just would exchange angry looks back at him, which he never saw but, Seti knew that I was upset about the whole thing. Seti still had those eyes of love, and I had those eyes of pure disgust. "How dare he even look at me like that after he shamed me" I thought to myself.

I remember one day, it was a grey cloudy day, Seti and Tuya were sitting on the balcony on some pillows with their three children; Ramses, Tia, and Henutmire. Seti said a few words to me and I didn't even respond, but look at him in hatred the very sight of him made me want to hurt him, but I knew the result of murder, especially if it's against the royal family. I remember quite well as to what happened to Beke, I didn't want to follow that same path. It was a chance that I wasn't ready to take no quite yet. But the day would come, and sooner than I was thinking it would be.

As Ramses got older, he got spoiled, perhaps even more rotten than his mother. Seti could tell that I didn't like Ramses, as well as everyone else who saw the young prince was a spoiled brat. Every time we would cross path, I would scold at Ramses and when he would make smart remarks I would make one back. This was my way as getting back to Seti for hurting my feelings. Another incident where I completely ignored the pharaoh was when we were on Seti's boat. I was sitting on the far side of the boat totally not paying attention the commotion of Seti and his son was doing in the back. I was in a completely different world, a world where Seti and his son didn't exist. Even to this day, when someone would do something to really piss me off, I would use the ignoring mechanism, pretending like they never existed to me, it works, and individuals mad, just how I want it. I know it's wrong to do that, but I have to admit, I'm still learning.

It pained me one night to be in the same room where he and Tuya were making love. I wept to myself. I tried to cry quietly, but the pain was too great, I couldn't keep such a pain inside any longer. My loud whimpering stopped the royal couple from making love each other.

"What's wrong Amenhotep? " Seti asked popping up from the bed looking down to me. I said nothing just got up from the floor and went home.

That day came when I've finally gotten so fed up with beings Seti's servant. Seti ordered me to fetch something for him, "No" I refused. This act shocked everyone in the room, probably even Seti even more. "You will do as I say" Seti pointed his finger angrily at me. "No" I repeated, standing before the king giving him stern stares. For my acts of disobedience, I was demoted as a slave where I worked on finishing the King's temples with his other slaves.

For hours, I've worked endlessly alongside the other slaves and when I fell behind, I was whipped. The king and his cohorts stood on a far balcony laughing and snickering at me, mocking me with harsh words. My sisters watched helplessly as I was being tormented by the guards, I could tell that they wished that they could have done something, but in fear of Seti's wrath, they did nothing. Finally, when I had enough of this torment, I refused to work anymore on Seti's temples.

My actions, again, got me whipped, but this time by Seti himself. Seti had me stood up. Bounded by my hands and my feet with my back faced to the Seti. As he whipped me, the Seti demanded that I look back him, and each time I refuse. The more I refuse, the more the whippings got worse and worse, I could hear the pain in Seti's voice when I refuse to even acknowledge him, it was almost as he wanted to cry. Seti's crackling voice didn't made me gave in to him; I stood strong accepting my beatings. Finally, when I couldn't take any more of the whippings, I slowly turned my head towards him signaling that I had enough of the whippings that I could even bare.

Satisfied, Seti walks away with his family and his cohorts while the other guards and my sisters unchained me from the stones. Feebly, I fell to my feet in pain. The scars on my back stung really badly, so bad that I could barely stand up. Despite the pain I was feeling, I was also teaming with more anger and tears.

That night, Mery and Ankh were cleaning my wounds, which still stung from earlier. Seti came to our home to see how I was doing. Again, I did not answer him. I kept my head turned from him on the pillow that I was laying on; my heart still cried out for him still, I was still intensely in love with him. After Seti, left I started to whimper very quietly trying not to show my defeat or pity in front of him or my sisters. I cried not because of the wounds but because I once loved him and the betrayed me in the most awful way,

"Enough is enough"

One night, while I was home with my sisters, relaxing, and chatting with Neferneferuaten Tasherit. A guard came knocking at our door. The guard came for me and said that the Pharaoh has sent for me. So, I followed the guard to Seti's palace. When I arrived at the palace, King Seti was sitting alone in his throne room fidgeting with a small figurine in his hands. The guard leaves Seti and me alone to chatter in the throne room. "You called for me?" I asked Seti responds "why have you forsaken me?" I replied, "I have not forsaken you" I'm assuming that Seti wanted to know why I was acting so distant and rebellious towards him. After that brief utter of words, there was a brief silence between the two of us. Finally, Seti dismissed me back home. I left the palace feeling content. Despite it not showing, I was still hurt about what Seti has done to me.

    Seti swore the reason why I was acting so distant towards him was because of Tuya. Seti probably assumed that I was jealous of Tuya, but I was far from it. It wasn't Tuya that I was angry with it was him. Seti caught me on the balcony just staring in the blackness of the night and joined me, attempting to make a conversation with me, but I didn't want to hear his voice. "We are not together" he implied suggesting that he and Tuya had a divorce. I knew full and well not to listen to anymore of Seti's lies, so I walked away from him leaving him standing on the balcony.

Even though I didn't believe a word that Seti said, he may have been actually telling the truth. Queen Tuya was no longer around as much as she used to. Still this wasn't enough for me to fall back into Seti's arms. Thus, in that moment on the balcony this would be the last time that I would see the pharaoh, at least for a while.

That night, I got an idea. My idea was to leave Seti's city for good. Early the next morning, I got up, while everyone was asleep and pack most of my belongings, and left the city. I didn't know where I was going to go, but I didn't care where, as long as I got out of that city, away from Seti and everyone else that was connected with him, as far as possible. I left not making a sound so that none of my sisters were alarmed that I was leaving. Before I left, I took one last gaze at Seti's palace, at the balcony that was connected to his bedroom, hoping that none of the guards sees me leave and hoping that the king won't see me leave. Finally, I left leaving my sisters and everyone that I befriended behind as I ventured into the desert. As I looked back on this moment, a part of me felt as if I was trying to return back home to my mother ,because I tried to remember familiar land marks that I've seen on my way to Egypt to find my way back to Mitanni, but I was unsuccessful. Instead, I was going the opposite direction towards Nubia. Nubia, as it was originally called was a country south of Egypt it is now known as modern Sudan.

As I stepped further and further into the desert, I wondered what would become of all the monuments and other works that Seti and I created over the years, but then I got a hunch that all of our works would be okay even after we were long gone. Thus, my worries were no longer needed.

Along my way from Egypt, I came across travelers. These travelers caught me off guard while, I was still crying over Seti. Apparently their wagon was stuck in an opening in the ground, the travelers tried to helplessly to pull this wagon out of this crack in the ground, but the wagon wouldn't budge. As I came across them, the male traveler asked me to help them pull out their wagon.

I tried to help them, but I only made matters worse. Not only was I unable to pull the wagon out of the whole, I also sunk it deeper into it. The man argued about this. "I'm sorry" I apologized repeatedly, as I got up slowly from trying to pull their wagon out of the crack. Finally, I gave up and walked away and walloped away in self-pity and tears into the desert.

For days, I've wondered that desert with little food, or water to support myself. In my mind, I've battle the thought of going back home but then again, I thought, I knew what going back would lead to, so I ventured on. When I couldn't take any more steps, I found myself on my knees crying out "God" begging for his mercy and he, whoever he was at the time, heard me because I regained my strength and the ability to walk again was restored. The desert hounds grew near howling in hunger. Not wanting to get eating by the desert hounds, I ran as fast as I could towards a nearby village that was at the end of the desert.

As I got closer to the village, I was captured by two very dark skinned men. I screamed at the top of my lungs, but it was useless because there was no one around to help me. The two men took me back to their home village and along with others whom they robbed and captured along the way. I was afraid for my life and thought they were going to kill me, "I was done for" I thought. Little did I know that I was in for a bitter sweet surprise when we arrived to their tribe area?

These men took us amongst other men whom viscously had their way with us. Afterwards, to our surprise, they did not kill us as their rules implied them to do. We each were given new clothing and jewelry by these strange people, as our old ones were torn up by the shameless men. These people, that I was amongst, looked and dressed a lot different from the people back home. For one thing, they were darker, some were even black, like the crayon and dressed in jungle like attire, you know like people from an African tribe. I didn't know who these people were, but they were far from being Egyptian. My guess, was that these people where the Nubians whom lived south of the Egyptians.

It is my belief, that we caught the interest of the peoples that led to our survival. Of course, I surely didn't mind, because I didn't want them to kill me, or anyone else that was caught for that matter. Upon him having his way with me, the son of the tribal leader grew feelings for me. At first, I didn't trust him and was afraid of him, because what he just got through doing to me, but he eventually grew on me, like Seti did.

My new found Nubian lover was fairly attractive, in all ways. He was built like an ox and mighty like a lion. He was a true warrior, possibly more so than Seti. Seti and my new lover had many things in common. My new lover was also someone, which I've come to know in this life. Like, in his present life, he was very cunning and humble, just like Seti. My Nubian lover was a bit shorter than the Pharaoh and taller than myself. My new lover was a brave man, born and raised to be a warrior possibly from his father the tribal leader before him.

The both of us connected instantly. We shared everything with each other. This included my reasons for being in the Nubian desert, the secrets that my sisters told me about Seti, his connection to my father, my family, and what I wished to do someday, to seek my revenge on the pharaoh. My new Lover totally understood and offered to help me, considering how he despised the locals of Upper Egypt. My lover also wanted to take their riches as well. This was start of a beautiful friendship between me and him.

As time went on, I've grown more and more to the customs of my new found home and even learned how to crop. At last, a place where I didn't have to obey orders, or assists rude royals and nobles. I was free from my bondage in Upper Egypt, but still very extremely upset with Seti, I was still waiting patiently for the day I would have my revenge on him.

Upon a grey and gloomy day, an unexpected visitor came to seem, my sister Ankh. "Ankh!" I said stunned as I was cropping. My memories never made clear as to how my sisters knew where I was, but it was possible that I kept in contact with them by letters. Ankh came in a hurry to tell me about our sister Neferneferure and that her sickness has gotten worse.

Immediately, I stopped cropping my miniature garden and journeyed back home with Ankh, despite my decision not to. When we returned home, we found Neferneferure crouching over on the ground holding her stomach in her hands. From the looks of her face she was in great pain. Not knowing what to do, I went to the man whom possibly knew what to do, to Seti.

Upon re-entering this old place that I haven't set foot in in so long, there was a sudden quietness when I entered the room. Seti sat amongst many women in his throne room. All of the women were startled by my sudden presence. One of his daughters moved closer to her father quenching the right arm of his throne. "Seti" I pleaded to him "I need your help". "Why should I help you?" he screamed at me angrily. Seti's face was so intense, I never saw him so angry like this before. Yet, it didn't matter to me because any feelings that I had for Seti, been gone and all that mattered was Neferneferure's life. "One of my sisters is sick and she need some help" I cried. Seti sat in thought for a brief moment and then commanded one of his priests to get medicine so that my sister can be healed from her sickness.

After giving my sisters the medicine, that Seti gave me to help Neferneferure get back to health, I ventured back to Nubia. But, as I walked on home Seti came along riding on a white horse after me. Picking up speed, I ran as fast as I could away from the king. Seti managed to catch up to me and held up his hand so that I could get on the horse but I refused to get on. I kept on running, picking up pace until finally, Seti stopped in his tracks and road off back to the palace. It's like I said earlier on, I made up my mind that I was never going back to Seti and I wasn't

On a sunny day, Seti and his soldiers came down to Nubia to discuss with their leader, my new friend's father, about plans to build temples on their land. Seti's sudden appearance was totally unexpected and Seti must have saw me earlier when I was attending the crops, plucking out cabbage, because before he and his men rode off, he stopped right behind me and spoke a few I believe his words were "why are you living with these Nubians" I didn't turn around nor did I said a word.

The Pharaoh wanted me to return home with him. Again, I refuse to go along with him. I was very comfortable being here amongst the Nubians. There was no chance in hell for Seti to get me to go back home. My mind was long made up before he got to Nubia. No way, was I ever going back to being a tortured and heart-battered servant. Shortly after, Seti's failed attempts to take me back home, the Pharaoh road off in his chariot back home. After Seti left, I took a deep sigh of relief.

Shortly after that, Seti left the village, angry and upset, my Nubian friend he came storming out of his father's hut. "What's wrong?" I ask my love, "What did Seti say?" My love told me that Seti wanted to build monuments in this area, in which we were living in. For Seti to want to build temples on the Nubians territory and remove their homes was terrible. How can he even ask to do such a thing? This bitter news thickened my hatred for the Pharaoh. "Who he thought he was to come here and take control of the Nubian's land?" I thought. My lover refused to allow him to take over their land, so he rallied up several other Nubians to rebel against Seti. My love's first plan was to invade the Pharaoh's palace. For me, this was a perfect opportunity to get back at the Pharaoh, and get my sisters out of Egypt, out of their servitude as slaves under the Pharaoh.

I told my friends everything that they needed to know about Seti's palace, from every passage way to every exit. The plan that my Nubian friend made was completely perfect in my eyes, and it would work just fine too. We were also preparing for battle in the temple we were all ready to go up against the Pharaoh; I think I was even more ready than everyone else. The plan was set in motion, and we drove off threw the night to Thebes. Coming on this journey was, The Nubian prince, his best friends, myself, and two of my close female friends. Together, we rode to Egypt, ambitious and battle ready, eager to end Seti's life.

First off, the two women and I disguised ourselves as exotic dancers. The heavy set woman wore pink, my other friend wore blue, and I wore my favorite color green. Meanwhile, my lover and the others set out to steal the king's riches and waited for a chance to attack Seti. The plan was put in place and the three of us came posing as special guests, dancers, as presents from the eastern kingdoms. As we pranced into the throne room, I was kind of hoping that Seti would notice me so he could see what I've become and what he transformed me into. I wanted him to see me, to be hurt by what I was about to do.

Seti and everyone in the throne room were very amused by our dancing. Seti stood in a trance as we kept on dancing, moving our body in a hypnotic manner. I kept my eyes pacifically on Seti, giving him stern stares fervent to strike him.

As we got to the end of the dance, our other friends attacked the Egyptian guards, who were completely that were unalarmed by their presence, that's when we all attacked. Everyone, including Seti, was in complete shocked. As I revealed myself to the court, I noticed that Seti had a new slave but this time she was a woman. His new lover stood on the side of him in front of his right arm. She had huge eyes, shocked by this incident. There I stood, staring at her, disguised and in anger but not at her, but Seti. I felt sorry for the young girl, if only she knew what she was getting herself into with the king. Seti noticed this and smiled this made me even angrier with the king. Untouched, my friends and I fought and killed most of the Seti's guards in the throne room. As we made our escape, Seti ordered the guards to captured us

Along the way, I came to my house to rescue my sisters just before the other guards came looking for us. Ankh and Mery where much older looking, as if they were in their late forties or fifties when I came to get them. Ankh and Mery were sitting in chairs, while Tenta'aten and Setepenre stood beside and behind them all looked withered and tired. In my absence, my sisters had been moved into a more complex home. The house was white, longer, and better than our first home. Seti must have had them move into a more decent home for reasons unknown. "Amenhotep?" Ankh says surprised to see me. With little time to speak, I told my sister to come with me and I grabbed Ankh, old friends of mines, and everyone else who was dear to me, thus in bondage under Seti and took them with me to Nubian. Neferneferuaten managed to take many of our belongings with her, but the majority stood where they were to be lost in the sands of time for good.

I slashed my way through some guards to join up with my other friends. We all made it safely out of Seti's city, laughing and giggling about the scenario. As soon as we got back home, we celebrated our little victory. We had male dancers put on a great show that even my sisters, Ankh especially enjoyed, clapping and laughing as male dancers performed before her. In the mist of our partying, our festivity, all of the sudden came to a quick halt as Seti sent a messenger to us. We didn't know what the message said, but I think we had a hunch. This message was a response to what we had down earlier that evening.

Seti came again to speak with the Nubian Leaders. This time I was there. I came out my hut just as Seti arrived to our village, standing very close to my new lover. As I walked out of the tent next to my Nubian lover and friends, not once did the Pharaoh glared at me, but I could see fire was in Seti's eyes as he talked to the chief's son. Seti was very angry probably because of my rebellion. I have to admit, I liked every bit of the way he looked. I wanted Seti to feel pain just like the way he did me.

IREM: BATTLE BETWEEN LOVERS

Just a few months later, after our little cue attempt in Egypt, Seti wanted to battle with us in Nubia, which the Nubians reluctantly agreed upon. The lands agreed to meet each other in the area where Egypt and Nubia meet, in an area which I believed was called Irem. Yet again offered I offered my hand in battle against Seti. My Nubian lover trained me in the art of the Egyptian sickle swords.

My lover was rough on me. He had to be to get me ready for the fight against the Pharaoh. It was hard for me to keep up with him in the beginning. Eventually, I got the hang of using this powerful weapon and was ready for battle, more like ready to finally get my revenge for my family, and myself. I was ready to kill the man that broke and stole my heart, thus stomped it into the mud like a useless toy or pottery.

We all arrived in the desert, lined up side by side, in front of the Egyptians who were well prepared for us. The Egyptians had their spears and shield, carefully in hand. It was very cool and breezy in the desert, and also very quiet. Seti never gazed at me once which angered me even more; it was like I never existed to him at all. Both sides were present and more than ready for battle. Before we went into battle, our fight was planned out and it was supposed to have ended with my lover slaying Seti but thinks to my blind hatred, it didn't exactly work out as we planned.

The two leaders gave out the command thus both sides clashed in an epic battle. From my point of view, it appeared to me that we had the upper hand against the Egyptians they look as if they couldn't stand a chance against us. We were wiping the desert floors with them. However, our luck was about to turn slightly. My Nubian lover had discussed a plan to execute the Seti, he really had high hopes that this plan would work, but he was about to be sadly disappointed by my arrogance. Sense we had the upper hand on the Egyptians; I took upon myself to attack Seti. This was a choice that I was soon to regret.

From the distance, I could hear my Nubian lover calling out my name "Amun-re" a new name given to me from him. My Lover tried to stop me from making a big mistake, but I ignored him. Outraged by the horrors he unleashed upon me, and my sisters, I attacked Seti, vigorously with my sickle sword not giving Seti the slightest chance to strike back at me, as though it seemed. Seti stood blocking my every move with his spear. At last, he got a clean strike, and impaled me in the left side of my left rib cage. The pain was greatly, but I didn't stop there. I slowly lift up my sickle sword to strike again. Quickly, Seti slashed me with his sword across my chest, finishing me off. There in that very spot, I stood their dying and in complete shock. Seti slowly backs off from and quickly as my Nubian Lover ran towards him. Afterwards, there was complete darkness, as I blackout on the desert floor.

A moment later, I awoke to find that the battle was long over. I look up to find the Egyptians retreating back home. It appeared to me, that we had won our little spar in the desert but with a terrible cost. Many of my fellow friends lay slaughtered on the desert floor. One of my lover's very close friends was left choking on his own blood, as he died. Blood streamed out of his mouth like water it was a gruesome scene to be in. None of this would have ever happened, if I had just listened to my Nubian lover, if I wasn't so blind with anger and revenge. The next thing that happened, I and many of the wounded were being carried away in a wooden wagon made out of sticks. Severe pain seeped rapidly through my body; it hurt so bad, that I could barely move the left side of my body, and my chest was hurting badly, Seti had cut me deep, deep in my chest, and into my heart and soul. The war was over and we have lost all because of me.

When we arrived back to the village; word had gotten out quickly about our battle against the Egyptians and my foolish move that is now costing me to lose my life. All eyes were on me. I could tell that everyone was angry with me; some were very upset and wept over their lost. Those who remained loyal friends with me were concerned about my injury. My lover, especially, was deeply concerned about my wellbeing.

My final days were spent in my hut, hurt, ashamed, and heartbroken about what happened back in the dessert. My wounds have gotten very worse and infected. The village doctors tried their best to help my stab wound heal, but there was nothing that the Nubians could do, I was going to die. Before my death, I took one last walk around the village, holding my wound with my right arm, seeing all the happy faces of the people that I loved for one final time. I spent my last day stood up against my hut, weeping in sorrow over Seti. I soiled myself due to being paralyzed by the pain of my wound. Still, I couldn't move most of my body. A part of me knew that I was going to die in the hut, and I did. My death happened so quick and suddenly that I didn't even know that I was dead. One clue, was that the pain that I was having ceased.

My memories didn't end with my death; it took me further into the future to a few moments, years after my death. The first moment that I saw was the events that happened just seconds after I died. My lover crying next to me and everyone that was still friends with me. In my hut, I remained lying on the hut walls, but with tears still dripping from my eyes, blood dripping from my wound, and urine flowing from under me. My sisters repeatedly tried to get me to wake up, but I didn't respond back, little did they knew, that I was not in my body anymore, but standing next to them. Shortly, after my death life continued on for my Ankh got married to a fine Nubian man and they both left to Ethiopia. The vision led me to believe that Ankh is the founding mother of my current family. As for my other sister I believed went to work back in Upper Egypt for Ramses II. Mery married a high official there as well. It is unknown as to what happened to my other four sisters perhaps they decided to stay in Nubia where they were all free.

Then, I was shown Seti's future. To my surprise, Seti was still very much in love with me, so much so that it drove him nearly insane. On a gloomy night, Seti was walking about and saw a commoner that resembled me. Thinking that this commoner was actually me, Seti scurried over to the man "Amenhotep!" he shouted grabbing the man's arm. The commoner then pushed Seti to the ground and flees leaving the king in tears, but I don't think it was because of the incident, it was because of me.

Next, I was taken to Seti's last day of life. He was withering and was dying slowly in his bed, his three children questioned him about who he would give the throne to, then Seti responded "go find Amenhotep" as he slipped away.

Seti lived the remainder of his life not knowing that I was long dead by the time of his own death and there was nothing to find but my bones. (Laughter) I find it very ironic that in the end we both were still very much in love with each other. I guess the love was still there after all. Hell it is now, at least for me it is.

Lastly, I saw my lover and some of his friends sneaking around Seti's tomb. Before I died I've told them about Seti's tomb and how to get around inside the tomb. My Nubian Lover managed to steal the pharaoh's gold and treasures, but before they exit the tomb he beheads the king paying homage to me, to me his lover. My Nubian lover scripted Seti's corpse of its gold and jewelry and placed them upon me upon my burial, I guess it was his way to say that I deserved to be buried as king.

Granted the age I was when I returned to Egypt, and the time frame that all this occurred, I indicated that my mother and I left Egypt around year sixteen of my papa's reign and I, myself returned to Egypt during year four of Horemheb's reign, or at the end. But here's the catch, I never saw the king in a day of my former life. King Horemheb was the last pharaoh of the 18th dynasty of Egypt.

MY LIFE BEFORE

After the 18th dynasty fell out, the succeeding Pharaohs more pacifically, the Rammesides, more pacifically Seti and his father tried their best to erase my family from history, even leaving their names out of the official kings list in Abydos, the temple king Seti had built for himself and his Gods. Instead, the Pharaoh Horemheb was placed as the successor after my then grandfather Amenhotep III.

It is unknown how long king Horemheb ruled, but it is well claimed that he ruled for fourteen years. I believe that Horemheb had a relatively short reign about four years and one month not fourteen years thus just added the years of the previous kings and pharaohs.

"AFTERMATH"

Two or More Lives Later

"To my beloved Seti though we are worlds apart my love for you will never die nor cease I wish you a fortunate future and a beautiful afterlife, your once and true love Amenhotep."

The wound that Seti inflicted upon me is still with me to this very day, and I mean that. Literally, it still aches in that exact spot of my rib where Seti impaled me with his spear as if it's still very fresh. For years, I thought I was just having really bad cramps, but I know now that it's not, thanks to the psychic, Silvia Browne. I've learned from her that we tend to carry old wounds and sickness into our next life or across many lives, in which I think I have. Silvia never made it cl1ear why we carry these things into our other lives (or she did and I forgot) but maybe it's for us to find a cure or other words, heal in the next life. So maybe it's meant for me to heal in this life

After that day, I've became a completely different person in a since. To me, it was as if I embraced my former life as Hung-foot, but that doesn't mean that I've been walking around thinking I'm actually an Egyptian servant instead I embraced those old feeling that never shook off upon death. Occasionally, I've only told several people about this event some believe that it is true and others remained skeptical. It was not long after this when I too became a skeptic and placed this dream at the back of my mind. However, I couldn't resist the emotional pain that I received from it.

Just when things couldn't get any complicated, the person who was Seti I in my past life was in my present life. Why does destiny do this to us? Put us in that position where we had past relationships with somebody and we end up meeting up with them again. Where all those old feelings come rushing back into your soul, at the time, I didn't know why. But now I can say we that are so we could grow I mean why else would we be in the same room I know for educational reasons but there are so many reasons for everything. Like I said earlier, I'm really glad that God put us in that position.

Seti hasn't really changed that much in this life; well first off he's not the King of Egypt anymore but still very fine. The very next day I had class with the person who was Seti in my memories. Let me tell you, I couldn't look at him the same way I did before these memories. A part of me hated him for what he done to me in those memories and a part of me still churned for him. However, I didn't give myself the slightest chance to get to know the New Seti but I was a position where we had to interact with him. As I observed him closely he's still was very humble and not much of a talker unless it's important matters. While observing him from my distance, he's actually a replica of his former self.

My memories of him, as Seti, attracted me to this person. It was hard to be around this person knowing that we had a past life together. Carefully, I would watch what I did around him, not wanting to make a fool out of myself, again in front of him. Every time I would look at him, I've found myself giving him the goo-goo eyes and wondering what could have been, or how could I've prevented those events that occurred from taken place. This guy had me going crazy even in this life; I was losing my mind while trying to maintain my emotions at the same time. When you have love like that you can't just throw it away, no matter how long it's been.

Set-reincarnated would be sitting in front of me and I would get locked into his eyes and sometimes he would stare back at me. Seti-reincarnated probably thought "why the hell does this dude keep staring at me?" As soon as he would look up at me my whole body would shake oh what a terrible feeling that was. I usually end our little staring competition by rolling my eyes just to throw him off.

My soul practically screams out to the Seti-incarnated most of the time and since I was no longer going to see him around I became worried and concerned about him. Not a day goes by that Seti-reincarnated be on my mind. Seti-reincarnated was always on the brains, he was in my mind. My thoughts, my sleep he was everywhere in my mind. No matter how I try not to think about him, I always find myself thinking about him again. This also makes me sad because this person will never know how much he means to me.

Every time, I've crossed paths with this Seti-reincarnate, I always wish to tell him about my experience just to try to get some closure on this but no, I thought, it was bad enough he thought I was weird. Surely, I didn't want him to think I was crazy too. Sometimes I want to scream out Seti just to see if he would answer back just to get his attention again but I fail to get those words out of my mouth.

To be even more honest with you all, I did had a crush on Seti-reincarnated, but it wasn't long for those feelings that I for him to fade away. As a matter of fact, I had this slight crush the following year before these events occurred. No Egyptian memories ever occurred until late that following year and that song triggered those memories to show in my head. I was even surprised that he even showed up in those flashes." What the hell is he doing?" I thought as these memories unfolding to me.

Let me tell you. I had a crush on every good looking guy that walked or drive passed me but I wouldn't receive any visions of knowing them in another lifetime. The dreams I have about these guys are well a bit too explicit and graphic I once even thought of Set incarnated in that way but as soon as I got those visions I never ever thought of him in that manner ever again, I can't even get myself to think of him like that anymore I feel as if I'm embarrassing myself or something like that. I felt as if heck we did it in the past and let it stay there. Seti-reincarnate stuck out to me more than those other guys because of those visions and only those dreams. So, yet again, he has a place in my heart. So there, for those of you who want to rule this out as some sick twisted fantasy. This wasn't, I repeat in a soft hearted tone it wasn't.

"He will never know how much he means to me" I kept telling myself. It's sad but it's the god awful truth and to be honest I'm okay with that, we have to move on out roads of life.

Just to be even more honest about my past, I also had a crush on my Nubian lover for years before these events but I only one vision of him in yet another life time but it wasn't that serious. As a matter of fact, the fact that I had another lifetime didn't affect me as much as it did with Seti-incarnated the only thing that happened was that my feelings shifted from love hate to respect and honor. Heck, I still got some moves from the sickle swords if that guy was to remember his warrior hood he would have bested, that guy was a beast. Those visions changed my prospective and actions towards Seti-incarnated they changed my behavior completely. It is always someone that you are or were deeply in love with that straightens you up.

Now, Seti and I are in two different worlds now even though in reality we both are sharing the Earth. I'm trying to chase my dreams and also trying to find; peace, reasoning, love, and basically my way out of pain and suffering. As for him, I don't know where he is perhaps in a better place than me, I pray that he is. I think God for getting reacquainted with those two men, truly a great experience I had with them both, a powerful king and a mighty warrior.

Lucky me, I actually got a second chance to meet my sisters again, but this time we were not related. We all worked together at a local store called Dollar General. I've been working with the three of them for about three months before this experience and it never came to my mind that they were once my sisters in another life time. Ankh and Mery were now close friends in this life long before we reunited with each other. They were close like sisters which I found it to be very amazing that the two had reacquainted not knowing that they were sisters. Ankh-reincarnate have told me that the two of them have been through a lot together and I've found it very heart filling that the two of them had each other's back even in this life.

When everything started happening it was Ankh-reincarnate that I told first about my experience she didn't believe me, but she did say some of the things I've been saying were truthful in a sense, like for instance the part of her and Mery reincarnated being like sisters. I laughed it off and I didn't expect her to believe me, neither anyone else at that time. The second person whom I told was Mery-reincarnate she smiled and said that "yeah we are kind of like sisters" Ankh-reincarnate was a sweet woman not and still very attractive she always kept herself up not one day she looked her worse. She would always keep her hair in a different style each week. Ankh-reincarnate told me that she likes to wear black hair or wigs because they make her feel good or something like that. This instantly reminded of the Egyptians, whom always wore black wigs. I didn't think much of what she said, because I was still in denial about the whole past life situation but as I thought about it more and more Ankh-incarnate was showing more and more of her former self to me, little did she knew. Just like in Ankh-reincarnates previous life, she was a woman of value. Mery-reincarnate and Setepenre-reincarnated both weren't a joke either. They always kept themselves up tight too with nice hair and nice clothes. These girls were bad, meaning they looked their best.

My sister's persona has changed a lot in their new lives. Compared to her previous life, Setepenre-reincarnate is far livelier than her former self. The new Setepenre was so cheerful and always kept a smile on her face. What a beautiful woman she turned out to be. Ironically, Setepenre-reincarnate was the next to the youngest person to be hired at Dollar General, and I was the youngest at that time, just how it was when we worked for Seti. I loved to I be around Setepenre-reincarnate she had this warming spirit that made you felt happy. When we were assigned to world in different stores I would always choose to ride with her and this other co-worker that I loved to be around.

You know up until recently, I always wondered who used to be my full sister Tenta'aten. It took me a year to figure out who she was when all in all, she has been staring me in my face all this time. I met my big sister again at Dollar General just like my older sisters. Tenta'aten was a regular customer at our store, who came in once every blue moon. She is still a very beautiful woman she has darker skin now but still holds some similarities to our mother. One night, all my four sisters were in one room. One night before, we were closing the store, Ankh and Mery was having a conversation with Tenta'aten reincarnate and a long one too. It was like the Aten him or herself shined upon my sisters.

The possibility of her being one of my former sisters slightly came to my mind when I looked back at them talk, while I was moping the floor, but at the time, since I didn't see her in my visions, I ruled that possibility out. When the three of them were talking it was almost like the room lit up it was like room was filled with great energy.

Sadly, Setepenre-reincarnates time came to an end at the Dollar General, as she went back to College. After this, I've only seen her but one time, and I never saw her again then not too long after, that Mery-reincarnate move back to her home state of Alabama. Mery-reincarnate always talked about her home in Alabama and how she missed it just like she talked about Akhetaten in her past life. Mery-reincarnate was missing home so much, that I partially encouraged her to go back home. Thus Ankh- reincarnates and I was left at the store. It saddened me by their departures especially Mery-reincarnated, simply because what I knew about her I pray to see my sisters every day hoping to get that reunion that I so longed for again.

My three eldest sisters and I still have a lot in common even today. We all wear glasses and three of us have the same complexion. Heck, on a few occasions a few people have asked Mery and Ankh reincarnate if I were their son, or were related to each other because we still looked similar to each other. "No" they would respond with a smile, I would sit back and smile about it thinking about those memories we shared together.

Due to the memories, my love for my former co-workers strengthened. Over the years, since we all separated from each other, I've grown to truly miss them as my sisters and the time that we had together. I'm just truly grateful that their reign of terror has finally ended, and that they are living beautifully as they so deserved it. My sisters dreamt of Freedom from their horrible previous lives. They would sit up late at night, when everything was quiet just to talk about their desires and wishes. Now, at last, it has finally happened. Ankh, Mery, and Tenta'aten has beautiful families and their living the life that they've always wanted, at least I hope

As for me, my time at Dollar General came to a demise I couldn't count when it came to the registers thus that led to my downfall and since then my life went straight to hell. But through those trials and tribulations, I've become more open with myself and to others, and even happier from within. The only thing that kept me down was not having someone I could talk to as a partner. Having a life time partner was my long time desire and seeing everyone else with one kind of saddened I and sometimes I've found myself doing awful things just to get some affection from someone. Needless to say, that shade of my life has faded away and I'm learning just to be patient. I was told just to be patient and it all will happen but not when you want it to happen but when God is ready for it to happen. Those exact words coming from the mouth of Beke and my other superiors. Man, am I'm glad to have ran into her again.

On the bright side, I'm still pursuing my desire to finish college. Having a decent living standard has become my main goal now "no more poverty for me" I kept telling myself but I will never forget the lessons that I've learned while being on my knees. I've learned to be appreciative for even the smallest of things in life. Later on, I realize that even if were to somehow get out of poverty my suffering isn't going to end for there will be more for me to learn.

Funny enough, Ankh and I found ourselves working at a different company but in different locations, ironic right? We both worked at Hardees. Ankh, as usual held a higher position than I did, but I was getting to her level. Ankh was and still good with her work. Of all my past siblings, Ankh was the one I was deeply concerned about the most. Every time I would walk by her house, I would wonder how she was doing. She made my day when she popped up in my stores drive thru and that was all I needed just to see if she was okay, and she was.

Because of my former sisters, I've become more so of an older brother especially to my baby sister, whom at which was also born the third child from the oldest just like Ankh. My middle sister is the only girl in my immediate family and I treat her like she was Ankh herself, plus I look to her as if she was Ankh. Now since she made me an uncle, I've become even more protective of her and my nephew of course. Just being around my nephew and watching over him, makes me think of the times my mother struggled to keep my alive in her present and past lives. I must have been a handful back then, I giggled to myself.

I feel that I owe my sisters, and Beke this story. All the time, I feel that it is my duty to tell the world about our trials and hardships after the downfall of our once royal family. It is because of my sister's sake, and my family, is why I wanted this story to be published so badly. To me, it was the least that I could have done after all that they've done for me. So Mery, Ankh, Tenta'aten, and Setepenre, this is all for you. I miss my sisters very much. Not a day goes by that I don't think about them. I imagine us all having one big huge reunion with all my members of my family, and their families because of this story. Each day, I wish that this could be possible so that I just could have one more day with my sisters, just one day out of the week.

The second person that I want to strongly acknowledge is my mother. My mother needs to know how strong and powerful she was as Queen Kiya. My mother needs to know that, all in all, she was something special, a force to be reckoned with as I would say. Compared to her present life, my mother isn't as strong as she once was I've even questioned myself yet again, was she really Queen Kiya? Man I wished that she could recall some of her memories so that she could uncover her hidden mightiness and beautiful that I feel that she feels that she have lost.

A lot has happened with me and my mother, so much so that we've butted heads, and even fought. It was either my attitude or the wicked deeds that she has done that kept us clashing like Titans. But, what it really was stress. My mother felt like she haven't lived up to her lifelong desires, and I wanted to fit and be loved. I was going through everything that a young gay teen was going through at the time. I got treated like and animal in those years from people who will never know the real me and it tore me up inside. There was some mental abuse and even psychical abuse from people, each other, but the worst part came from us, thinking less of ourselves.

That very moment when she walked out that temple, I felt like I lost her forever and in a sense, I did. I just want her to get well in her state of mind, and I'm hoping that I can bring her back to the glorious woman she used to be. It may sound crazy to you readers but sometimes it takes looking back on the positive things of your past to reconstruct what have become your shattered futures a little self-motivation from ones past achievements and altitudes to keep our heads up and looking on down the long path of life.

My entire family is even more important to me, thanks to these memories. Even though we are all set in our ways, it doesn't change the fact that we are family. Thus, Family should be down with family no matter what the situations is. It's true what my grandmother said to me "if I had to make the choices that I've made, you wouldn't have been here". I never had any respect for my grandmother, because I always saw her and everyone else as the enemies. However, now I understand what she was trying to express. If she didn't do what she did this peace of memo wouldn't have come out. So, therefore, my grandmother is one my biggest contributors to this book.

Overall, learning that bit of information about them made me honor these women. Those women looked after me once upon a time thus Ankh started my whole family line on my mother side of my family, I will forever be grateful for her and I will always love her as a sister as well as the others who were my sister. My sisters were and still are my biggest heroes because they took great care of me and saved my life.

To this very day, I still drift off worrying about my former sisters. I wanted to know how they are doing and where they were also if they were doing okay I even thought about Tutankhamen. Hmm, I thought, "I wonder who he is now or if he even was reincarnated like my sisters. Made me wonder will we ever cross paths again. In a way think I may have.

On December 5th 2012, I found myself reminiscing about my former life as an Egyptian servant. One day I came across two brown wooden bowls identical to the ones I use to carry around Seti's palace and temples. I smiled as I held the two flat bowls in my hands for a brief moment just thinking about my past life, which I've come to miss.

I was missing my former life sincerely. I missed my home in Egypt bad, and wanted to go back to Egypt, just for the nostalgia. Oh how I wished to go back in time and relive that life again, just that once I though. If only I could, I sure would but a little differently than I've lived it before. First off I would have taken the toilet, the tooth paste, a toothbrush, deodorant, soap, bleach and everything that makes you stay clean. Back to my past life I've looked back from those times and compared it to this time and am amazed of how far we, as in mankind, have come along but also saddened how we've become. We've become even more senseless and wicked than we ever were and it's tearing us apart. People are just getting more miserable than they ever were and that's a serious problem.

As I was trying to explain to Ankh-incarnate about my experience, she still said she didn't believe. "Well I believe that I was reincarnated" I responded to her one of her statements, "yeah and I was married to King Tut" Ankh-reincarnate implied. I paused for a moment, lost in thought while trying to count my register and responded by saying this "well maybe you were", I responded with a smile, "You never know what could have happened" I said. It actually turns out that she was indeed married to King Tut. At that time, I thought that King Tut's era was a whole different era from King Seti, like a hundred years apart or so. Never did I think that their reigns were closely linked. I've learned a lot of ancient Egyptian history because of these memories. My little sister said I should become an Egyptologist since I talked about Egypt so much. "Hmm" I thought, "maybe I should look into doing that one day" I kept on thinking.

Seti wasn't the only one that looked defined his wife, Queen Tuya still looked charming as she did in the past, I can say that for the least. Tuya-reincarnate is very gorgeous looking some of her old features have leaked into her previous life such as her fashion sense and her high maintenance. Everything but her unkindness wasn't there and that's a good thing.

Tuya-reincarnate worked at a BI-LO, right behind the Dollar general where my sisters-reincarnated and myself were working at. So in a way, we all were still very close to each other. Every time that I would go into Tuya-reincarnate's line to ring up my groceries, I always glare at her having that image of her as a queen and King Seti's former wife, thus the mother of Ramses the great. Like I said earlier, Tuya is now nicer. Although I'm not actually her friend, I'm someone who spit out a few good words to her, every time I cross paths with her. The notion of wanting to say "I use to hate you in a past life" would be at the tip of me tongue, but I don't want us to relapse in a rivalry between us again, oh no there's no need for continuum in that area.

At one time the former royal couple had crossed paths after three-thousand and something years now (or whatever). Little did the two of them know that they both shared so much in common together? It brought a smile on my face to see the two of them face to face, just inches away from each other giggling and laughing. When I saw two standing next to each other it brought a smile on my face and laughed. "Oh the royal couple is next to each other and they don't even know it" I thought, caressing my chin not to mention I was one the persons whose tail Seti chased, what a peculiar moment that was the three of us a former love triangle.

I've even pointed out Seti reincarnate to Ankh-reincarnate and she joked about my experience again. "Oh Pharaoh" Ankh-reincarnated teased and giggles repeatedly. In that moment, I thought about the way she was saying that, and said to myself "there was a time when you use to cry out that". Well, it was more like "you sure were crying out that when he was about to smack across the floor". Man, I wanted to tell her that but didn't want her to get smack across the floor. Ankh-reincarnate was a very reverent woman. In other words, she kept this child in his place. Overall, I was flattered by our little reunions and the fact that somehow we all managed to still be connected with each other. Boy was 2008 a great year (laughter).

My life was pretty complicated in those years past of 2008-2012, to be honest, I've had a rough life to begin with. I've went through so many drastic changes mostly due to my own stubbornness and impatience. However, somehow, through the mist of all the pain the memories of Seti and my former life slipped through the cracks without me even thinking about those times. I guess that was some odd way of reminding myself who I was and

Ever since this experience, I've looked at those who were with me at that time quite differently especially the person who was Seti. I always see them as who they were when I was Hung foot. When I see this guy, my body freezes in shock I tried not to make a fool of myself every time I see him I even tried to ignore him and ignore the fact that he was Seti. I always wish that I could get the guts to share this with him maybe someday just maybe I will.

Despite these thoughts of fear, these people always seem to bring a smile on my face. I was proud to know who they were and who they were now. I'm glad that God gave me a second chance to get reacquainted with these people, although our encounters were bitter, and I wasn't the friendliest person in the world, I'm really glad that I was able to see them again. I kind of wish I knew this earlier, perhaps our encounter would have been less nasty, and I probably would have been nicer to them. Like I said earlier, I'm really happy to have seen their beautiful faces again.

You know that ole saying "until we meet again" it really lives up to its message. You never really know when you might see the same person or persons whom you've come to love over the years. I believe that "the soul recognized the soul" meaning that you might recognize someone from before.

I'm really glad that I've got the chance to meet Seti, one of the many great kings of Egypt. I think the reason why we reunited is so that I could close that door that I left open in that life and I'm sorry to say it's still open and I'm not closing not until I reunite with Seti, the new him and tell him what I've saw. Maybe that way I could get some closure on these events

Up until recently, I'm finally living for me again. No more walking around with pitying myself and I just recently found out that those guys whom I believed were my older brothers weren't my brothers, all in all and I was hurting for no reason at all. What was my reliever was the episode *"Charmed"*. It was the episode where

Piper was crying over her eldest sister Prue's grave. Like, Piper I really felt like I lost my two of my older brothers and I needed them. But thank God, that he proved me that I didn't. After balling my eyes out to this episode every time I would watch it on YouTube, my depression was over. No more was I walking around with a grey sweater. That episode really healed me because I almost didn't survive that depression. God, I really wished they hadn't ended that show.

In a sense, those guys did big brother me because they helped me during my growing process. I've become a stronger older brother and a great provider for my siblings and I wouldn't have done it without them. I really want to think them for that.

Learning from my big sister Mery, I embrace being the eldest of seven children. I find it kind of funny how I was the youngest in that life not having a care in the world and now I'm thrown into the position of the oldest child where I have to be a positive role model for my siblings just as Mery was for me and my other older sisters in my life before. I think in all my lives I was the youngest and the Lord had to do something completely new with me. Perhaps, I'm here to teach my younger siblings how to be strong and courageous as I once was or our lord just decided to teach me a lesson in how to be responsible and trust and believe, I'm learning. A long time ago, I use to wish I had an older brother or sister to look up because I didn't want to be stuck with the heavy responsibility of being the eldest of so many children. But now, Tssh, I can take on this responsibility I don't need older brothers.

However, I still find myself thinking about one of those guys. Many late nights, I've stayed up, crying and wonder why would he watch over me like that, why would he do the things that he done, if I wasn't nothing but a faggot to him why did he care so much?, and what was it about me that draw his attention? Unfortunately, I will never get the answer to this but; little did he know that I cared so much about him too. Heck, that situation was also a hard learning experience for me. It taught me how to be very protective and grateful for the siblings that I have. I guess I have to think him and that other guy for that. A harsh storm has passed and there is calm, a calm that

I've haven't seen in all my years alive. Finally, there is peace in my heart and a love yearning to be ignited again.

My present sister, not too long ago had a baby boy, the next in our line as I like to call him. My little nephew came in this world in a hurry. Silently, to myself, I wondered why? What's the rush in coming back here in this hell whole of a reality we got down here? He's a brave soul to come down, or back here. It took my nephew being here to drive me even further to publish this story, because I was ready to say the hell with it and throw it all in the trash. But he and future Thutmosides must know that they all descend from powerful kings and queens. To be influenced by their ancestors just as I have. So, I guess you can say, my nephew came down here for a good cause to spread hope to a long forgotten, and ancient family.

MEHY: THE LOVE SONG

My connection

For a long time, I began to believe that just maybe there isn't nothing of me to find, perhaps Seti wiped me from all records but then there was this. I stumbled upon this love poem about a man named Mehy. Mehy was is some unknown being that existed exactly the same time I did, during the reign of King Seti I. it's unknown where his origin is from but its suggested that he is a favorite from outside the then royal family. Mehy also wore princely attire and was said to be a warrior. I was the descendant of many warrior pharaohs and I wore a tone of jewelry

"Could this have been me?" I thought no it couldn't but then again, I thought just perhaps it is. I started to think logically to myself if the same thing happened to Mehy referring to the fact that I hated Ramses II and basically sidelined after his birth led me with the conclusion that what I believed could actually be possible.

According to the records he fell out of favor and was disliked by Ramses II, Seti's the son. I believe that Mehy was just another nickname of mine and that this poem was dedicated to invoke Seti's love for me. It is stated that Mehy was supposed to be next in line for the throne but was sidelined due to the fact that Ramses II was around. The same exact thing happened to me as well which concluded that I was once Mehy. So just maybe after all, I did leave a mark in history.

MUSIC TO MY SOUL

Sometimes, good music cans sooth the soul

> "I recall the days; the days when we made love I can still feel the heat when we shared each other. Don't you feel the magic the mystery's in the air let's go down to lovers lane to the LOVE WE SHARED"
>
> —*Mary J Blige "Reminisce"*

Like Mary J. Blige, I was rolling in my bed at night tossing and turning having Seti soaring through my mind. You should have seen me; I was killing that song in my sleep. I imagined seeing Seti standing before me reaching out to me. Reminisce was right on point to from note to note on every thought and sweet memory I had about Seti. My mom was a serious fan of Mary J. Blidge and I never thought I would too the girl know how to reach you in all of her songs.

    Like many old souls, I jammed to music that too mature for me simply because I could relate to those songs more than modern songs you here on the radio. To get rid of the heavy baggage that I got from these memories music was my only solution to deal with my problems. Every time I was going through something, I would turn to music more than I would pray, yeah I know that was a bad thing to do but I'm sure the good Lord will forgive me. Amongst Mary J Blidge, Tamia also was one of the artists whom songs helped me get over the worse of the pain. For instance, her song "Loving You Still" helped me get over the emotions I felt when I was traveling through the desert that song hit every feeling that I was going through at that moment. The line, "I had someone watching over me, my protector" hit me the hardest. For me, it was true, because Seti always looked over me and held me by his side at least until that fateful day when I love was no more.

Just as I was going through this past life recall, Tamia had a song called "Almost" which was to me was related to what I was going through. Just like Tamia, I was recalling things, times, and place that I have never been too in this life and times with a person that I never was involved with. You should have seen me; I was acting up to this song, meaning I sang the hell out of it in my mind. Tamia has helped me get over a lot of the hard painful parts of this experience. I still listen to that song just to keep the memory fresh to tell others of my experience. Thanks Tamia!

But as soon as I gotten over my experience, here comes these s songs that rained upon me that made me remind me of my past life again. Every time I would hear a song that was even related to Egypt, or the pyramids, I be like "all oh lord give me a break". But I guess the lord was saying "Oh you need to remember this" but why? Why is it so important to me to remember this? Soon afterwards, I discover why. I've found myself tossing and turning over these thoughts with the song "*Dreamin*" but Vanessa Williams. Oh, sometimes it would be agonizing to sleep especially with that song playing in my head, making me go back to those memories, but it helped narrow down my thoughts of this life.

"I'll be dreaming in, dreaming hoping you'll be there." I would be dreaming about Seti's temple, (all the time) my sisters, and especially Seti completely lost to the melodies of Vanessa William's song.

No song hit close like Fat Joe and Chris Brown's, "Another Round". I remember when I first heard this song I laughed about it and said to myself "Oh shit" here we go again, rolling my eyes. The songs had already caught my attention because how it beautifully sampled my favorite classic Troop's "I will always love you". I always wondered when someone was going to sample that song and always thought it would have been nice if it was made into a rap song and what do you know, it happened, what were the odds of that. I still laugh at how that came to be. Another thing that also caught my attention was the spears. Now remember that I got severely injured by Seti' spear.

I was singing "Another Round" mostly because I wanted to have another round of Seti, but to me the song was made for his point of view, because it was him who was torn between two or more lovers, but in the end only he knew who he wanted. In a sense this, song told my story before even I could share it with you, and I found that very peculiar. It might sound strange how a song would play a role in all this, but trust me if you were going through what I was going through, you'll be like "damn" too. This song always takes me back to my former life when I was Amenhotep, and I listen to it just for nostalgic purposes, heck I've probably listened to this song about a thousand times (or more) and has never gotten tired of it. It's now signature to my memories.

Majority of the time, I listen to old school R&B, because old school R&B are more affective, and they get to you better than some of music of today (there are some good new stuff don't get me wrong, but the old music is better). One of My favorite old school singers was Tina Marie. For about a month or two, I had the Tina Fever. Tina's music had me rocking in my sleep all the way to my bones. From her "Square Biz", "Loving" to her "lover girl" I was rolling even in my bath tub, but one song really caught my attention was her "Deja Vu. On a grey day, in my apartment, while I was trying to put this story together, Tina Marie's "Déjà vu" played on the radio. When I first heard the song I was shocked. "A soul song about reincarnation?" I said to myself "what?" I didn't even know that such a song even existed but one sure was playing on the radio.

The song instantly hit me due to its truthful lyrics. I used to be many things, many surprising things whether a woman or a man.

I'm truly grateful to be a man but it wouldn't matter if I came back as either or. This wouldn't matter to me, because I will love my skin no matter what shape or form it's in. Also I believe that it's all part of the good lord's grand design for us to be reincarnated not to just die and wait for judgment day that's so boring.

Sometimes, when I thought about the memories, a song related to Egypt would come on the radio. One time, I was strolling down the isle of Dollar General, my old work place, to get some tissue while thinking about Seti a 80s rock song about pharaohs and Pyramids played on the store radio. I was utterly surprised and laughed about the song. "Aaah again" I said to myself chuckling as I went up to the cash register "give me a break" I pleaded to the lord above. That incident seemed bizarre to me but dead on point in what I thinking about.

Speaking of Dollar General, I ran into Seti incarnate there. It was about two years since I last saw him, Seti still looked as handsome as ever and I looked tired and well just leave it at that. I tried to hide in the isles of the store not wanting him to see the way I looked and the way I was living. Back then, it terrified me to have old class mates see me down in the dumps but eventually, I allowed it to be known that yes, the boy who thought he was this and that, wasn't at all. Soon, I got out the isles and we up at the cash registers I was left side and he was on the right. I waved at him, but he said nothing back. Oh well, I thought, I'm assuming that I deserved that. I never let down how mean I was to him in High school, but I felt like I had to, to throw him off and everyone from ever getting close to me. I scared of them being tapped into my horrible life I was living at the time I took precautions and being mean was one of them. However, Seti-reincarnate was a jerk when I first had class with him, but still it wasn't my reasons for being mean to him.

Dancing always helped too. The song that I always clicked on was "I Can Go Deep" by Silk. Why this one? Well, I was trying to go back to my dancing roots, because I used to dance to songs like this when I was Amenhotep. Even now today, I still love to move my body. Songs like this kept always keep me churning. I even pretend that I'm dancing in front of Seti, when I'm dancing to this song and envision his smiling face pleased at my pirouetting. Sadly, I cannot dance like I use to because of my wound that ached every time that I would move my hips.

I'm a big fan of Silk by the way I absolutely love them. Another favorite of mine from them is "Lose Control." This song is so touching and for me became poetic because I was losing my then and now over Seti. I was also burning with the desire to know more of my past life at the time which drove me even more insane. Every time this song would play, I would drift off back in time singing my heart out.

"LET ME LOOSE CONTROL!" I sing to and from and to work" SETY, LET ME LOOK INSIDE YOUR SOUL!" I cried out. Ooh this song got to me to the point the I was even humming the opening lyrics in my sleep. It's such a nice R&B classic.

I've found myself singing Pebble's always saying "Seti, I love always", just singing my heart out. By the way, I'm not a very good singer. Yeah, I know it seems as though I was going out my mind, but I was going insane out of love, a love that has lasted for over thirty-three thousand years between me and an Egyptian ninetieth dynasty Pharaoh. Our love will continue to last even after this life I'm in. I dare myself to find something that could compare to the man Seti was. I have yet to find that someone that could come even close to him. At some point at night, in my dreams I've found myself saying "just one time", "just one last kiss from Seti" wishing to have one more last moment with him. Just maybe, I would get my chance again, just maybe. But, until then I could only dream about it.

Ever since this experience, I've become obsessed with any and everything that has to do with Ancient Egypt, especially, if it has something to do with the Amarna Family. I've become hungry, practically starving for answers to this possible past life. Indeed, I've found some, but there are still some mysteries that have yet to have been unearthed to myself.

I truly believe that this was one of my many past lives. You can call me crazy all you want, but this is what I believe. No one really knows what happens to us when we die, absolutely no one. To me, life is one of the greatest mysteries to mankind. No matter how science can prove its functions many of its greatest secrets will forever remain a mystery.

This experience has changed my entire perspective on the concept of life after death, Karma, and the spiritual world. Even though I'm open to these three subjects I'm very afraid of at least two of them, karma and life after death. I'm trying hard not to do wrong to someone with the fear of karma coming back and biting me on the butt or having to pay for my crimes in the afterlife or in other words, my next life, if I will have another one. Personally, I don't want to come back because people are just plain miserable down here and they are rubbing it on ever one else. But, if the lord wants me to come back to teach others the lessons that I've learned, I will, but other than that, I don't want to come back.

My advice to you readers is to be very careful how you treat people whether it's big or small matters because even the very little things count. Also try not to go out for revenge because vengeance could only lead to your very own downfall as I learned as Hung Foot. Finally, be forgiven of one another and set aside differences I assure you'll be on good terms with karma.

MOVIE MADNESS

Before the visions, my interest in Egypt was due to the movie the Mummy (1999) with Rachel Weiz and Brandon Frasier. I was so intrigues by this movie and how it made the ancient world so exciting. When I was younger, it scared the crap out of me, but as I got older I became more and more in love with it. Strange enough, the character that I liked the most was Ankh-sen-amun, the lover of the antagonists Imhotep.

I was always drawn to this character and it felt like I knew much about queen Ankhesenamun. It never occurred to me that I may have once known the actually real queen, either that she was my once my sister. Since the movie I was walking around as portraying as if I was actually an Egyptian royalty as if no one could touch me and even imitated some of the lines from the movie.

It always amused me how movies about Mummies and Ancient Egypt would be so well written and thrilling. Even the actors and actresses do a great job in playing their roles. Speaking of movie stars, I think a good actress to play Queen Nefertiti, if someone were to do a movie on her life, would be Angelina Jolie. The two have so much in common, except the jealously part. The two are very positive role models. I admire Angelina Jolie mostly because of her work as Goodwill ambassador of the United Nations High Commissioner of Refugees; I think that's awesome what she does. Angelina often reminds me of Nefertiti in essence, which kind of made me wonder sometimes if the two might have been one and the same in the past. But, I wouldn't know for sure my view point of Nefertiti was always distant and never in close encounters.

The Prince of Egypt (1998), what a movie. It is the movie that made me fell in love with the story of Exodus and of Moses; that and the Ten Commandments (1956). My favorite part of the movie is when Moses leads his people out of Pi-Ramses and the lead females began to sing and at the end of their song the little boy starts to sing it practically brings me to tears but it's the duet with Mariah Carey and Whitney Houston that really shook me out.

For the past five years of my life, I've been lost in the wilderness. I was Jobless, homeless, and flat out depressed. My situations would be so excruciating, that I didn't think I would make it out of them. This led me to believe that I was destined to fail at everything I tried to be good at and it left me feeling like I was a loser. Sometimes, I've found myself asking the lord why did you bring me back here and to take me out. I just had no hope for myself and was very doubtful and this song and a lot of inspirational songs gave me wings to fly out of all that.

My love for Seti was what brought me back to this childhood movie and this heartwarming song. This wasn't the first time that a Whitney Houston song or movie gave me some inspiration. Her "Shoop Shoop" (my favorite) allowed me to exhale many obstacles and pain that I was holding on from years past. It's because of Ms. Houston and other good musicians that am able to smile again.

When I heard of Ms. Houston's death, I was shocked. I remember my mom calling me into the living room, "Terrell! look Whitney Houston died" I remember running into living and sitting on the arm of my mother's couch and moved into tears. Never has a celebrity has touched my heart, in fact; she wasn't just some celebrity to me. I felt like I lost someone that was close to me because a year later after her death I was still mourning her. It saddens me how her life ended the way it did but she's in a better place, I know it. Whitney was the only artists the really reached me with her music.

"There can be Miracles, when you believe though hope is frail it's hard to kill. Who know what miracles you can achieve when you believe? Some you will when you believe"
-Whitney Houston ft. Mariah Carey
"When You Believe"

STATURE OF PEACE

I would like to thank our father God and his good son our lord and savior Jesus Christ for restoring these memories within myself. I feel you wanted to remind me of what the consequences of revenge, adultery, malice could do to me and also to show me what a beautiful person I was and still am. Because of this experience, I now know that every human being on this Earth is entitled to struggle, it's how we grow spiritually and physically to become better human beings. I appreciate my struggles father and I Thank you both again for this beautiful experience.

To those, whom I've come to know, whether it be; friends, family members, foes, just people whom I've come across. Whether it was to give me a place to stay, or just words to heighten my gloomy days, I want to say thank to you all. Thanks for believing me and for also opening up your ears to listen to me.

I want to directly pacifically think Mrs. Alfrieda Deas Potts (Beke) for believing and allowing me to relook upon that light, which was slowly fading away from me. Had you not open your doors back then, I probably would have been washed up in the ocean, or half way around the country still trying to figure out how this life stuff works and words of encouragement has reopened the door of possibility and chances and the doors of faith and self-love, I think you for that.

Don't think I forget about you, Mr. Willie Potts. I always wondered what the hell you meant by don't leave before the miracle

I was like "what in the world you meant by that?" Literally for days I've sit and thought to myself, I wonder what in the world he meant by that and there I was sitting there for a miracle to fall in my lap. It turns out that I did leave before a miracle happened.

When I left to go off to Job Corp, I felt as if I wasn't doing the right thing with the choice I made as if I was pushing something a side that I could have and it turns out that I did. Finally, I know what you mean by that thanks for being the positive role model and father figure in my life so much change has happened because of you and your wife thanks for being there to listen in my time and need.

To Isa, my first uncle figure. Man I always loved when you narrowed me down to the real stuff and told me about myself you pushed a lot of crap out of me that was just sitting on my chest I can literally say that you and the Potts took away the feeling of wanting to fie away from me. Isa I hope you continue to deliver the truth to young knuckle heads like myself. No I ain't gonna lie to you; there is much for me to still learn so my head hasn't soft up just yet.

Hye Lisa, My favorite librarian. Thanks for believing in me and seeing something in me when almost no one did, and also giving some words of inspiration and support because I needed them. Your right, you always have to have faith. What is faith when there is doubt? Those two doesn't work well together like oil and water.

Don't think I forgot about you Mrs. Thelma Miller. You were my Yoda, my mentor, and the person I would run to whenever I needed some advice I has learned quite a lot from you. I will never forget that day when you ask me for my help. That day changed my life, and that's why I always came to your house to see just how you are doing. I will never forget all that you have taught me and I will take all that I've learned from you with me on this continuous journey to my destination, thank you dearly for all that you've done for me. I wouldn't have made it out alive if you weren't there to support me. I think you dearly.

Once again, I want to thank Omm Seti for giving me the strength I needed to put this thing out there. It's a shame that we never were acquainted in the past and even in this life but perhaps someday we will. Maybe we might reincarnate as best friends if so I can't wait. Rest in peace Ohm Seti and may we meet up again in the afterlife.

Lastly, I want to think all my teachers from K-college. Even though it seemed like I wasn't paying attention to you in class, it turns out that I actually was. Every day of my life, I've taken what I've learned from school and implied it to my life. Thank you for helping me embraces my talent in written, and allowing me to do now. I wouldn't be a sufficient author if it wasn't for you.

These people, man they were their when no one else would even care to bother. Yes, I've burned my bridges in the past, but I don't regret none of it because in the end, as I've always said, something good came out of my downfall and I'm glad that everything happened the way it did because I wouldn't have matured like I did.

Lastly, I want to thank you readers for also opening your ears to listen to me as well. Remember, be careful how you treat others in this life, you never know when it might come back to bite you in the behind. Also remember that this skin we are in is only temporary, and your time here is on a fixed time. So use your time wisely. Be wise and always defeat evil with love, and great kindness. Don't get caught in its illusions because you'll get lost in it, with that I leave you this message. Until we meet again, love Terrell.

It's true, there is absolutely no way to prove my former existence, or that my story actually happened and there probably will never be proof. But, one thing for certain, that my father loved my mother and they had a love that extended from not just one child. Though it may not look that way, it's evident. My father didn't dub my mother the favorite for nothing. Even in their separation, my parent's love was still very there.

We think we know what's going to happen to us once we get to the other side, but the truth is that we really don't. The only way we will ever find out is when we get there. Everyone believes that three things happen to you when you die. Either you go to heaven to eternal peace and happiness, hell to agony and suffering, and purgatory, where you have to wait for judgment. However, there is a fourth choice, reincarnation.

Many times, I've been questioned by mean and nasty skeptics. They always asked" If reincarnation is real, then what the point of us coming back on Earth?" the answer is simple, it's to learn. I swear to you, I was a lost soul before this second experience with reincarnation. It took me learning more and more about my past self, how powerful and beautiful I was in essence to make me more mature. Thanks to this experience, I've found myself again thank you again God for this wonderful experience.

One time, I was literally told that reincarnation wasn't real, but I had to remember this powerful quote that the lord told me when I had my ear full of Skeptics. This is what the lord told me "Who are they to tell us what is real and what is not? Did they create the moons and the stars, the tides, and all the lands? I think not. For they are liars and deceivers and don't truly believe in the power of God.

What I took from this message, was that the Lord was trying to convey that there is no such thing as impossible. I mean come on, God can anything he (or she) wants to do, so why can't he bring us back a few times so we can learn a few lessons? I rather suffer on earth than in hell. Heck, its hell living here on Earth if you really want my opinion.

Not everything from the past is bad. Sometimes it's those good memories of one's self that gives us strength to push forward, thus to make more fond memories in the future. Memories that I've had that you want to keep for a life time and over.

There's a song that I like to listen to by an artist known as Jon B. The song is called *"Time After Time"* from Jon B's *Bonafide* album. I love to listen to this song because it takes back to those tender moments with Seti. One time, I've dreamt of our reunion. Seti stood on the far side of a desert just waiting for me and as I walked I hear" Time after time" playing in the back ground as I walked slowly to be reunited with Seti, finally closing the door on or sorrows.

"Time after time, I'll be yearning for you" I sang quietly to myself and I found myself just doing that. You all can say that this was a fantasy neatly drawn from the back of my mind and you can call me insane but I know how I felt and to me that, that's one of the biggest parts of this story.

A part of me is still in love with Seti, and a part of me wants to move from this experience. Yeah, it's shocking, but it's the truth. I truly want the best for Seti-reincarnate. I really want him to find that woman, I said it, woman, because like my guard lover we are two worlds apart. I hope he find, or is with that special woman that is fit for him, to catch him when he falls, and to hold on to his arms, just as I did many lives before and I know he will.

To Seti's future lover, Please treat Seti well because that man has a very good heart and a great soul. I wish you treat him with kindness and don't take his love for granted. Because a deep love experience like the one we share in our past lives, is hard to come by these days. I wish the two of you can share the same hugs and kisses that we also shared in a time before and a chance to wipe each other's tears. So be kind to my former love please, that's all I wish from you be mindful and be well.

There is one song that I want I've song to myself to keep my spirit up, it called "I was here" by Beyoncé Knowles. I've kept repeatedly singing this song, not just to tell everyone and myself that I was here in a past life, but I am here now as well, and here this is my story that way people can remember that I was here. My version of the song is in past tense saying that I've done all those things that the singer said she did

"I have left my footprints on the sands of time, knowing that there was something that I left behind. When I leave this world, I leave no regrets. Leave something to remember so they won't forget. I was here, lived I loved. I was here, I've did I've done. I did everything that I wanted and I found out that it was more than I thought it would be. I have left my mark so everyone would know that I was here."

I've caught myself in liberation of the whole situation happy to have the experience that I had. One night I came home dancing and singing *"Do You Remember the Times."* I was doing all the dance moves and Egyptian dances from the music video I was enjoying myself that night. I was having more fun that I having in a long time, I even insist some of my close roommates to come dance with me. It really did feel very liberating that night.

" Do you remember the times, when we first met" I sang out loud " Do you remember the times, when we fell in love" loud

"Do you, do you" I bobbed my head back and forth sideways having lots of fun and filled with boundless joy.

"Yeah I remember." I repeat to myself repeatedly, laughing and giggling.

In those moments I felt a sharp pain in my soul and a deep one in my heart that almost brought tears to my eyes. This pain wasn't of sadness, it was happiness, happiness that I lived and I live and these lives brought me to love and know so many beautiful people I will never forget it, it's a story that I will tell my grandkids(I have any) and so forth.

One very last thing, I would like to say one thing. We are free to believe in whatever we feel. Don't listen to those people, who tell you that these things that you believe in aren't true, or do not exist, or is wrong because they will try to make a fool out of you. In reality, they are the true fools, and they do not have an open mind. Excel in your own mind; allow it to be open up to many possibilities not negative ones though.

Right now, I'm waiting just waiting for the day for someone to prove that my story is actually real, and all this happened to me in a past life. I'm hoping that this book can be very beneficial to archaeology and finally close the door on the mystery of the Dynasty, but until then, I will be at home patiently waiting. See you all in the near future.

Hopes for a Bright Future

If my story would ever become a movie in my times, I would love for singer Tyrese Gibson to play as the Pharaoh Seti I. Tyrese looks somewhat identical to the ancient king and has some strong Ramesside features. I think if anyone is deserving of this role it would be him. Also, I think to play his mother Sitre-In who else but the woman who I believe was her in the first place, Angela Basset. To me, it would be like she's playing herself, well a former part of herself.

When I saw *Black Panther* and saw how Ms. Basset was playing Queen Mother of Wakanda and praying to the goddess Bastet I was like look at her playing a role that she didn't know she was familiar playing. As you can tell she is one of my favorite actresses of all time. Who else could play her but the woman who used to be her and I think Angela Basset would bring this Ancient Queen to life on the big screen because she was her in a time before. In opinion, I think that actress Naturi Naughton would be good to play Seti's wife Tuya.

As for my sisters, Meritaten, Ankhesenapa'aten, and Setepenre, I always thought it would be cool to see Janet Jackson (Meritaten), Sanaa Lathan (Ankhesenpa'aten), and Lauren London (Setenpre), play as them. The Amarnan woman were extremely beautiful charismatic and these ladies are just as that. Janet reminded of Meri because she was a spearhead in her family and wasn't so much of a talker in her early years just as Meritaten but she, like my eldest sister was a prominent driving force for her family and I think if a movie was to be done about the Amarna Princesses I think Janet and Meritaten would be fun. Granted that my sisters were in their late 20 to 30s by the time, I returned to Kemet, Janet Jackson and Sanaa Lathan doesn't look at day or age pass forty and I think they would pass 100%.

As for my almost identical sisters Neferneferure and *Neferneferuaten-Tasherit* I always thought that the twins Tia and Tamera Mowry would be perfect play the two Amarnan Princesses because their strong bond reminded me of Nefernerfure and Neferneferuaten-Tasherit. It would bring me great joy to see these girls play these two little known princesses and even acting again, I enjoyed seeing these two-acting growing up in the 90s. *"Sister-Sister."* Is one of my favorite childhood classics and its actually because of the twins and the show *Moesha* that inspired me to want to go to college in which I did. One can only hope in dream.

If this movie were to be made within my lifetime Lupita Nyong'o would be my choice to play as Tenta'aten. Even though there is little to no information upon the daughter of Kiya historically, I still would like for people to know that she once existed. Much like majority of the daughters of Nefertiti it appears history has forgotten her, and I hope that this could change. Afterall, her story is my story and she is just as important as the other princesses.

As for Nefertiti and Queen Tiye, I think Viola Davis is the only actress that could take on the role as the formable Queen Tiye. She's such a strong actress and Tiye was such a powerful queen it would be a dream come true to see this happen. Queen Tiye had many daughters and it would be interesting to see who would play seven of her daughters. Sometimes, I imagine Jennifer Hudson playing as Sitamun *"the sitting princess"* and the eldest daughter of Tiye. (laughter) Man, I've played this imaginary movie in my head repeatedly so don't judge me. As for Nefertiti herself, who else but Queen Bey to play the role. Now I'm not much of a Beyonce fan or Bey-crazy but as the years went by I felt drawn to this artist. What drew my attention further to the Legendary performer is when she paid homage to the ancient Queen in the 2018 Coachella.

It warmed my little heart to see her pay homage to my late ancestor. Not too many people could channel Nefertiti and she did so. If there was a future movie made for Nefertiti despite my own Beyoncé would be my choice. Yeah, I know, I've gotten way over my head, but one can dream. It would also be an honor to see members of my family and the persons who helped shaped this story to be also join in on making this story come to life.

"I've been called a monkey and nothing more than the product of slaves. True, my ancestors may have been slaves, but I believe in my heart that my family which comprised of the 17th and 18th dynasties of Egypt once ruled and dominated ancient Kemet."

If this movie would ever come to be in the near future, I would like for everything to be right and precise to the time of the late 18th dynasty to early 19th dynasty of Egypt. From the location down to every even that led to my previous death. THERE WAS NO NEED FOR WIGS FOR THE AMARNA WOMEN. All my sisters were extremely beautiful and had long following wavy hair except for Tentenaten who had always sported the Nubian wig just like my former mother Queen Kiya. After the fall of the Amarna Dynasty the surviving daughters and children of Akhenaten did not live lavishly or in fairness after the collapse of the 18th dynasty and this I want people to know because from a historical standpoint everyone from the family just died off and I want to tell the entire world that this was not so.

I'm not wishing for a star-studded cast I just want the persons who are best fit for the role as these historical figures. What I want people to take from this movie (if it comes to be.) is that the story of Amarna did not end with Tutankhamun, it ended with me. There was one more male heir to the throne but unfortunately, he did not make it far enough to secure a place in the throne. Seti and I were a force to been reckoned with we sculpted out many beautiful works of art and temple, some in which was unfinished. Had I been not caught in my feelings Egypt would have been in the palms of my family yet again, but the higher power had another destiny in store for us. Despite, the bloodline has survived into modern times, my maternal family and I are living proof of this. One day, I hope, that this story is told, and I hope that it done correctly and in the right way.

Only time will tell where this story would lead to and I'm hoping that it would lead to many great things in the future., especially for my family's sake. I'm hoping that with this book that my family's course of history could change and yet again more prominent figures would rise up from my family and keep our name sake strong. Whether or not that this comes to pass one thing's for certain that the royal bloodline still and forever will live on within my descendants and their descendants as well and that is one fact. that the Priests of Amun cannot erase.

"Though my body and these bones are new, this soul of mine is old for I am young and old at the same time."

-Terrell Frazier

GLOSSARY

Here is a list of important figures from Ancient History, whom I shared a lifetime with. Here are some brief biographies of these interesting people.

Akhenaten: originally known as Amenhotep IV was a pharaoh of the Eighteenth Dynasty of Ancient Egypt. He was the husband of the famous Queen Nefertiti and believed to be the father of the famed king Tutankhamen. He was the first Pharaoh to break away from the original traditional gods and establish that the Aten was the main god in his reign. This caused a great religious upheaval during his reign and caused him to get in trouble with the cult of Amen Re.

Akhenaten: the city built by Akhenaten during his reign. This cites is now known as Amarna.

Amarna: Also known as El-Amarna it was the home of the Pharaoh Akhenaten and his family.

Amenhotep: an ancient Egyptian name which meant that "Amun is satisfied". It was common around ancient Egypt and many of the Eighteenth Dynasty kings were named Amenhotep

Amenhotep I; was the great grandfather of Amenhotep the II, and an ancestor of Akhenaten and Tutankhamen.

Amenhotep II: Father of Thutmosis IV, great grandfather of Akhenaton.

Amenhotep III: The father of Akhenaton and Grandfather of Tutankhamen

Ankhesenpa'aten: The third daughter of Nefertiti and Akhenaton it is believed that she was King Tutankhamen's Great Royal Wife and half-sister. She served as Tutankhamen's co-regent Ankhkheperure Neferneferuaten in the beginning of his reign.

Ankhesenpa'aten Tasherit: a mystery princess whom shares the same named as Ankhesenpa'aten, she later changed her named to Ankhesenamun during her husband's reign to unassociated herself with her father's Aten cult. She was married to Tutankhamun.

Aten: the Sun Disk, it was worshipped by the Pharaoh Akhenaten and his wife Queen Nefertiti in a brief history in Ancient Egypt known as the Amarna Period. In this time, Akhenaten cast aside the old gods such as the Chief God Amun and placed the Aten in the forefront. The caused religious suppression all over Egypt and after Akhenaten's death his religion also died.

Ay: Former priest and successor of Tutankhamen. Ay was thought to be the father of Nefertiti. He married Tutankhamen's widow Ankhesenamun to gain claim to the throne.

Beketaten: Akhenaten's youngest sister she is believed to also be Nebetah under a different name. Beketaten is also thought to be the mother of Tutankhamen.

Gildukhepa: The secondary wife of King Amenhotep III and the aunt of Tadukhipa

Great Royal Wife: is a term used to describe the chief wife of some pharaohs as some Pharaohs are known to have more than one wife. The Great Wife's roles is more important that the lesser wives.

Hennutaneb: Likely the third or fourth daughter of Queen Tiye.

Hittites: were a group of people that were amongst the rivals of the ancient Egyptians.

Horemheb: Former General under Tutankhamen and the Boy King's original successor until he was outmaneuvered by Ay. Became pharaoh after Ay and therefore was the last king of the 18th dynasty.

Iset: Or Isis was the second of third daughter of queen Tiye. She was either the third or second princess to actually marry her father Amenhotep III.

Juni: the mother of Tadukhipa, wife of King Tushratta, and the Queen of Mitanni.

Kiya: Kiya was the secondary wife of the Pharaoh Akhenaten and his favorite wife. Kiya was once thought to be the mother of the infamous boy Pharaoh King Tutankhamen also known as king Tut. She is believed to be a foreign princess known as Tadukhipa.

Mehy: an unknown figure from the time of Seti I possible Hung Foot the secret male lover of King Seti I under a different name.

Meketaten: The Second daughter of Akhenaten and Nefertiti whom died due to a foodborne illness

Meritaten: Akhenaten's first born daughter and Eldest sister of King Tut and Queen Ankhesenamun

Meritaten-Tasherit: a mysterious princess born with the same name as the eldest Princess Meritaten its likely she's a cousin of the Amarna princesses and princes

Mitanni: is an ancient north eastern civilization that was just north of Egypt it once served as an ally to Egypt during the reigns of Amenhotep III and Akhenaten and various other Pharaohs

Mutemiya: The mother of King Amenhotep III, and a minor wife to King Thutmosis IV. She is the grandmother of Akhenaten and the great-grandmother of Tutankhamen. Like Queen Kiya after her she is said to hail from Mitanni.

Nebetah: Younger sister of Akhenaten. She is also the daughter of Queen Tiye and Amenhotep III.

Nefertiti: the Great Royal wife of Akhenaton who is famous for her beautiful bust.

Neferneferuaten-Tasherit: the fourth daughter of the Pharaoh Akhenaten and Queen Nefertiti.

Neferneferure: the fifth daughter of Akhenaten and Nefertiti

Nubia: a country within the lower regions of Egypt

Nubians: name given to those inhabiting the area of Nubia.

Ramses I: the father of Seti I, the husband of Queen Sitre and the grandfather of Ramses the great. He is the patriarch of the nineteenth dynasty of Egypt

Ramses II: also known as Ramses the great the third pharaoh of the ninetieth dynasty. He was the second son of Seti I and his wife Tuya. He is said to be the biblical pharaoh in the Exodus that refused to let the Hebrew people go.

Rammesides: referring to the Pharaohs whom names where Ramses or was associated with a pharaoh named Ramses. King Seti I am amongst these Rammesides.

Reincarnation: the belief that one is reborn again as a different person in another life time

Seti I: The second King of the 19th Dynasty of Egypt. Seti I. is the father of Ramses II, who is also known as Ramses the Great.

Sitamun: the eldest daughter of Queen Tiye and the first to marry her father and become a Great Royal Wife.

Sitre: also known as Tia- Sitre, she was Mother of Seti I and the wife of Ramses the great. She was also the grandmother of Ramses the great

Setepenre: the six and final daughter of Akhenaten and Nefertiti.

Setenupe: A cousin of the eight Amarna Princesses and King Tutankhamun she is likely a daughter of Iset one of the princesses aunts and some unknown male

Smenkhare: Smenkhare was the co-regent of Akhenaten during his final years as King.

Tadukhipa: a foreign princess that was married to Akhenaten she is thought to be Queen Kiya, Akhenaten's second wife. She was niece of Gildukhepa.

Tenta'aten (or Tentenaten): was the daughter of the minor queen, Kiya and Akhenaten. She was the half-sister of Meritaten, Meketaten, Ankhesenamun, Neferneferuaten-Tasherit, Neferneferure, Tutankhamen, and Setepenre. Her name meant "she of the Aten." She was the couple's first born child.

Thebes (Egypt): was the name of an Ancient city in Egypt. It was once the capital of Egypt in the ancient times it was home to many Pharaohs.

Thutmoside: this refers to all the kings and Queens of the Eighteenth dynasty. Thus four of these kings being named Thutmosis.

Thutmosis IV: the father of Amenhotep III and the grandfather of Akhenaten thus the great grandfather of King Tutankhamen. His name meant "He of Thoth"

Thutmosis V: the eldest child of Amenhotep III and Queen Tiye. He was the Crown Prince of Egypt and was supposed to succeed his father on the throne as the Thutmosid line ascension suggested but he died young and his brother Amenhotep IV aka Akhenaten became the next heir to the throne.

Tia: The wet nurse of Queen Ankhesenamun, the wife of King Tut. King Seti's mother also was originally named Tia as well.

Tiye: Wife of Amenhotep III thus the Grandmother of King Tut, Meritaten, Meketaten, Ankhensepaaten, Tentena'aten, Setenupe Neferneferuaten-Tasherit, Neferneferure, Tutankhamen, Setepenre, Ankhesenpa'aten Tasherit, Meritaten Tasherit and Hung Foot. She is the mother of Thutmosis V, Sitamun, Iset, Nebetnehat, Henuttnaneb, Akhenaten, Nebetah, and Beketaten.

Tutankhamen: supposedly the son of Akhenaten also known as the "Boy King". Was the only Pharaoh to have his tomb perfectly intact he is also known for the alleged "Mummy's curse." Tutankhamen's name means "the living image of Amun" it was originally Tutankaten "the living image of the Aten."

Tuya: the wife of Seti I and the mother of Ramses the Great.

Tutshratta: The former King of Mitanni the father of Tadukhipa and the brother of Gildukhipa, Tadukhipa's aunt

MY LIFE BEFORE

"Who are we? Are we the skin we live in? Or the hair we wear? Or even the shoes on our feet? Or are we something greater that's one of the greatest questions in life?

-Terrell Frazier

www.ingramcontent.com/pod-product-compliance
Ingram Content Group UK Ltd.
Pitfield, Milton Keynes, MK11 3LW, UK
UKHW022225230426
12048UKWH00016BA/1070